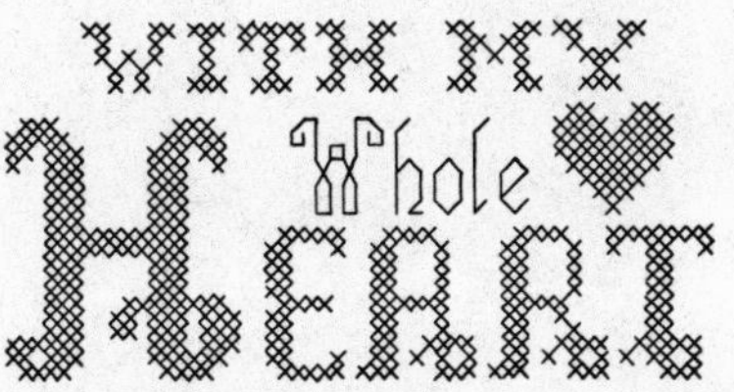
WITH MY
Whole
HEART

Karen Burton Mains

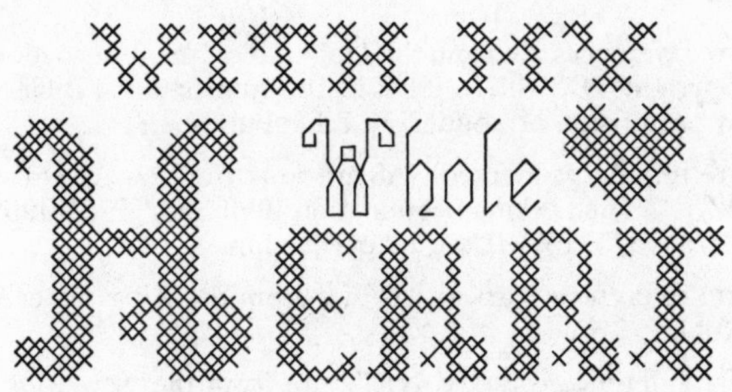

With My Whole Heart

Disciplines for Strengthening the Inner Life

MULTNOMAH · PRESS
Portland, Oregon 97266

Scripture references are from the Holy Bible: New International Version, copyright 1973, 1978, 1984, by the International Bible Society. Used by permission of Zondervan Bible Publishers.

Scripture references marked NAS are from the New American Standard Bible, © The Lockman Foundation 1960, 1962, 1963, 1968, 1971, 1972, 1973, 1975, 1977. Used by permission.

Scripture references marked KJV are from the King James Version of the Bible.

Scripture references marked NKJV are from the New King James Version, © 1982, by Thomas Nelson, Inc.

Cover design by Lois Kent Davis
Edited by Liz Heaney

Multnomah Press is a ministry of Multnomah School of the Bible, 8435 NE Glisan Street, Portland, Oregon 97220.

Printed in the United States of America

Library of Congress Cataloging-in-Publication Data

Mains, Karen Burton.
With my whole heart.

1. Spiritual life. I. Title
BV4501.2.M3285 1987 248.4 87-11297
ISBN 0-88070-197-8 (pbk.)

87 88 89 90 91 92 93 – 10 9 8 7 6 5 4 3 2

CONTENTS

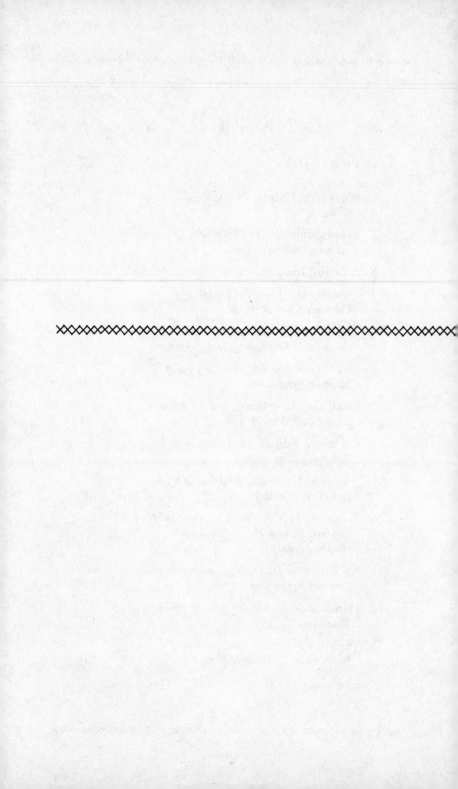

I'M A BIG GIRL NOW

When the Public Broadcasting System telecasted *The Jewel in the Crown*, I was intrigued enough to read the epic work upon which this series was based: *The Raj Quartet*. Paul Scott's four books portray the panoramic sunset of British rule in India during the years surrounding World War II.

One character in particular captivated me—Sister Ludmila, a woman of obscure origins who some people in the Indian city of Mayapore thought crazy. Scouring the streets looking for the dying, the starving, and the diseased, Sister Ludmila was a woman of spiritual substance who directed and funded the Sanctuary, a hostel for the poor.

At the end of Sister Ludmila's life, an interviewer attempts to jog her memory about a crime which had taken place years earlier, the centrum around which the plots in the four volumes range. Blind now and infirm, answering the questions by means of a rambling dialogue, the old woman talks about the contemplative life her physical disabilities have forced upon her and about her relationship with God.

She tells her questioner: *"I'm sorry about your eyes,* He said, *but there's nothing I can do unless you want a miracle.* No, I said, no miracle thank You. I shall get used to it and I expect You will help me. Anyway, when you've lived a long time and can hardly hobble, about on sticks and spend most of the day in bed, your eyes aren't much use. It would need three miracles, one for the eyes, one for the legs, and one to take twenty years off my age. Three miracles for one old woman! What a waste! Besides, I said, miracles are to convince the unconvinced. What do You take me for? An unbeliever?"[1]

I like that.

Much of my life I have prayed for the instant incredibilities; miracles for the unbeliever in me, if you please. But the Lord is attempting to teach me another kind of prayer, prayer for the already convinced, prayer that has no verifiable answers.

Prayers for peace, for the halting of the demonic possibility of nuclear destruction.

Prayers that clear the way for food to be distributed to starving nations.

Prayers for national spiritual regenesis, that the hearts of Christians worldwide will be turned again toward their first love, Christ.

Prayers for those who are held (in the vernacular of an ancient phrase) "in bitter thralldoms."

There are simply no measurements that will verify if these prayers are having any effect. Hours are set aside simply because God has asked me to do this work (without the poof! boom! bah! of foreseeable results). This kind of prayer requires the spiritual stability and inner doggedness which is described in Philippians 4:4-7:

> Rejoice in the Lord always. I will say it again: Rejoice! Let your [forbearance] be evident to all. The Lord is near. Do not be anxious about anything, but in everything, by prayer and petition, with thanksgiving, present your requests to God. And the peace of God, which transcends all understanding, will guard your hearts and your minds in Christ Jesus.

This is a description of the Sister Ludmilas of the world: women whose minds are filled with the presence and personality of the Almighty. Women who are aware that he can do whatever he needs to do. Women who understand that after years of obeying God with their whole heart, Christ's mind finally inhabits their own. Women who do the task at hand without needing lengthy explanations of whys, whens, or wherefores. Women who can say, "Three miracles for one old woman! What a waste!"

These mature Christians understand the spiritual dynamic explained by a well-known evangelist who said, "The older I get, the quieter God shouts." They understand, but they don't complain. God no longer has to work a miracle for them to believe. They know that his presence is miracle enough.

These are Christians who are spiritually grown up.

I distinctly remember when I realized God was asking me to grow up spiritually. One Christmas I wanted to give my Lord a gift of a three-day fast. I have been a self-indulgent, overweight, middle-aged female and have always had difficulty with the discipline of fasting. But this particular Christmas I wanted to say to him, "I'm giving you this fast for you to use in whatever way you deem best." Wonder of wonders, not only was I strengthened to keep a total food fast for three days, I surprised myself and extended this to four days. A first in my spiritual journey!

I'm a Big Girl Now

On Wednesday mornings it was—and is—my custom to slip into a nearby Episcopal church for an early Eucharist service. Taking the elements seemed to be an ideal way to end my gift-fast. There were just a handful of us present, and we stood before the altar to receive the bread and the wine. I hadn't eaten for four days; I felt lightheaded and my stomach was woozy. I was beginning to do more than sympathize with the starving of the world. But I rejoiced inwardly at my milestone spiritual achievement. I had been able to give my Christmas gift to the Lord! I expected a miraculous word from the Scripture readings, something akin to "Well done, good and faithful servant."

One of the readings for that morning, however, was from Hebrews 10, "You need to persevere so that when you have done the will of God, you will receive what he has promised. But we are not of those who shrink back and are destroyed, but of those who believe and are saved" (10:36, 39).

That scriptural word, paraphrased by the Holy Spirit to my heart, was *Oh, come on Mains! Stop patting yourself on the back! You're way behind on your spiritual development. Don't wallow around in self-praise. Keep at it!*

The simple truth, which he knows and which I am suddenly coming to realize, is this: I am a big girl now. It is time for me to serve God with my whole heart. It is time for me to grow up spiritually.

In one year, Christianity lost three holy women of faith, Agnes Sanford, Corrie ten Boom, and Catherine Marshall—as well as countless others whose names are unknown but who nevertheless did the work of God in this world. These are the women who knew what it meant to experience the presence of the unseen, who spent hours on their knees, who wept over the wounds of the world. For them, prayer was a second language. Who will take their place?

Frankly, there are very few candidates from our generation of women—those of us who have lavished hours in front of the television set, in the shopping plazas, in self-indulgence, in not developing a disciplined spiritual life.

Unless—unless, we begin to grow up spiritually. Unless we become convinced that we are the generation of Christian adults ultimately responsible for the spiritual condition of our nation. We must understand that there are increasingly few in that generation ahead of us left to pray over this world. We are coming of age. But are we coming to terms with our lack of spiritual depth and ability?

It is we who must learn the meaning of forbearing.

It is we who must develop the disciplines of spiritual perseverance, not shrinking back from growth but doing the will of God, having faith, and keeping our souls.

It is we who must become women of faith and prayer and obedience and service.

It is we who must set a spiritual standard for the next generation.

It is time for us all to grow up.

This book has been designed to help you do just that. Each chapter discusses an inward discipline of the spiritual life that has hastened my own spiritual growth and if applied will do the same for you.

Although conveyed in the vernacular and costumes of our twentieth-century, these inner disciplines are classic in their roots, historic and time-tested as to their efficacy.

Susannah Wesley, the mother of John and Charles and an amazing spiritual mother for us all, once said, "I am content to fill a little space if God be glorified—but I want to fill that little space well." Death is not creating little spaces needing to be filled, but gaping black holes in the network of spiritual alliances. So many seem content to let them gape.

Recently I have found myself praying, "Lord, I would rather die than live a life that would in any way bring shame to you." I find this prayer is not original. Jeanne D'Albret, who lived from 1528 to 1572, was the daughter of Marguerite, the queen of the little-known kingdom of Navarre, located in the northern flank of the Pyrenees. The mother worked tirelessly for the cause of the reformers while remaining herself a Catholic.

The daughter, Jeanne, went a step further and proclaimed Calvinism the religion of Navarre. This was at great price since France was still strongly Catholic and the passions of the time were hot and deadly. When her enemies tried to keep her from attending services of a Calvinist minister, she declared: "It is not my purpose to barter my immortal soul for territorial aggrandizement."

Living through a long period of religious wars, she threw her fortunes into the support of the Huguenots and was in constant personal danger because of her work of religious reform. She declared Calvinism the religion of her province and decreed that in places where Catholicism and Protestantism were equally followed, the churches should be used jointly by both worshippers. She encouraged the study of theology by large grants, and her son Henry became King of France and was able to provide religious liberty to Protestants in the Edict of Nantes. Jeanne died at the age of forty-four surrounded by rumors that she had been poisoned by Catherine de Medici, the queen-regent of France. In her last prayer she said: "Deliver me . . . so that I may offend thee no more."

Women like this are our predecessors, our progenitors, the spiritual bloodline of our female lineage.

It is time that we like they, through rigorous discipline or by standing for what we believe, be prepared to suffer for our faith. It is past time that we grow up spiritually.

1. Paul Scott, *The Jewel in the Crown* (New York: Avon Books, 1979), p. 129.

Editor's Note:

There are self-examination questions for individual study or group discussion at the end of each chapter. A study group can work on one discipline a week with interaction occuring during the discussion time, or an individual might prefer working on one discipline per month with interaction through daily life, experience, and personal prayer. The prayer at the end of each chapter is meant to be prayed consecutively, either twice a day for a week or once a day over a thirty-day period as a means of internalizing the chosen discipline. The prayers have also been printed in the back of the book for the express purpose of being clipped out so that you can carry them with you.

1

WASH YOUR HANDS:

The Discipline of Inner Cleansing

"Wash your hands!"

What parent or grandparent or teacher hasn't said these words to some child?

How many mealtime prayers have been delayed because a parent has had to say, "Son, I think you better go wash your hands . . ."even when washing hands before meals was understood to be standard operating procedure?

And what child hasn't balked at least once at these instructions?

Wash Your Hands

Strangely enough, though washing hands may be onerous to a child, water-play is a favorite pastime. I can remember my children spending hours at the kitchen sink with plastic cups and miniature figures and water—dripping, sloshing, pouring, splashing, overflowing. I can remember the towel dikes I built, lining the edge of the counter so that the water would not drain past these fabric dams; I remember the wet cuffs of shirts and blouses, finally rolled back. I remember the utter watery bliss.

As far as our kids were concerned, bubble bath, big sponges (for squeezing), and empty dish detergent squirt bottles were standard fare for baths. Although a child might protest having his head washed, he could spend endless moments with the plastic wind-up water toys—whales that spouted water, boats that chugged through bathtub lakes, little swimmers in painted suits whose arms rotated in unlifelike fashion in the water.

Getting a child into the tub could be a chore, but getting a child out of the tub could be a chore as well.

How well I remember teaching a child how to wash his hands. I remember the chubby fingers and little palms, a miniature rendition held between my own. I remember rubbing the bar of soap, washing all four hands at the same moment, and then rinsing them under the running water.

I remember the clean hands and face, the still dirt-streaked neck and wrists, and the bathroom towels stained with residue from too-hasty washings. I remember dirty denims in a pile on the floor, and grubby knees and matted hair and baby shampoo. I remember the miracle of that beautiful cherubic body all clean and soft and new; and the great terry towel smelling fresh from the laundry; and wrapping a child—hair and limbs washed, sweet and compliant now—in the folds.

"Tra-la! Tra-la!" I'd cry to my child in his terry cloth royal robe, "Here comes the King! The King! The little King!"

Sometimes we'd make bologna sandwiches. The recipe is as follows: Take one well-washed child (about standard pillow size). Place one pillow on the bed—the first slice of bread, and put one chunk of bologna on the bread. (We preferred the Mains's brand, but any small child will do.) Sprinkle with imaginary mustard, ketchup, onions, and a pickle—a sustained tickling motion is best for applying condiments. Add the top slice of bread (the second pillow.) Pick up and hold both pieces of bread and bounce until the squealing bologna falls to the mattress.

I remember the magic feel of a washed child in clean pajamas. I remember the summer sprinkler sessions—a great substitute for evening baths and having to clean the bathroom.

Washing my children brought me intense pleasure.

Our Heavenly Father takes intense pleasure in the washing of his children, too. He's a parent who continually leads his children, soiled with the world, to the laver. He plunges our hands into the basin of water; we protest, "But I was playing!" Like any good parent, he teaches us how to become clean.

I often repeat these refrains from Scripture:

> Who may ascend the hill of the LORD?
> Who may stand in his holy place?
> He who has clean hands and a pure heart,
> who does not lift up his soul to an idol
> or swear by what is false (Psalm 24:3, 4).

A variation on this theme is found in the short chapter, Psalm 15: "LORD, who may dwell in your sanctuary? Who may live on your holy hill?" (v. 1).

In other words, *Daddy, whom will you allow to sit at the dinner table with you, in your house where you live?*

The answer is:

> He whose walk is blameless
> and who does what is righteous,
> who speaks the truth from his heart
> and has no slander on his tongue,
> who does his neighbor no wrong
> and casts no slur on his fellow man,

who despises a vile man
  but honors those who fear the LORD,
who keeps his oath
  even when it hurts,
who lends his money without usury
  and does not accept a bribe against
    the innocent (Psalm 15:2-5).

It would take a lifetime for theologians to exposit this passage in such a way that their hearers would really begin to live out these instructions. But I think for the purposes of this book we could summarize the answer: The one who washes her hands will eat at her Father's table.

Have you washed your hands? asks the Parent.

The child who has bathed, who has cleansed the inner person of the soul, is the one who is welcome to come close to her heavenly Father, to crawl into his embrace, to laugh in the intimate joyful play that goes on between parent and offspring.

Sometimes we don't wash because we're afraid we will bring down our Parent's wrath. We've been playing in the forbidden mud. We hear the imagined words of anger and judgment from James 4:8: "Wash your hands, you sinners, and purify your hearts, you double-minded."

We forget that in his Sermon on the Mount Christ preached "Blessed are the pure in heart." We forget that the Father God is always calling us to cleanse ourselves. "Wash and make yourselves clean" he says in Isaiah 1:16-18. "Take your evil deeds out of my sight! Stop doing wrong, learn to do right! Seek justice, encourage the oppressed. Defend the cause of the fatherless, plead the case of the widow." Then follow these magnificent words, "Come now, let us reason together . . . though your sins are like scarlet, they shall be as white as snow; though they are red as crimson, they shall be like wool."

God delights in the spiritual bathing of his earthly children and he wraps them, cleansed, in the wooly towel of his love and approval.

Spiritual awakening always begins with cleansing. It begins in the heart of the individual who suddenly says to himself, "I'm dirty." And that is painful, particularly if we've been pretending all along to be clean. We go kicking and protesting to the water basin—we'll give our faces a swipe, but we don't want to wash behind our ears. We need to remind ourselves that as children we relished waterplay . . . that it's wonderful not only to *be* clean but to *smell* clean . . . that pure joy can be experienced in the bathtub . . . and that we have a Father who loves it when we wash.

F. Kefa Sempangi has written a book titled *A Distant Grief*.[1] It tells the remarkable story of the church in Kempali, the capital city of Uganda, during the reign of Idi Amin. Despite the intense persecution of Christians, this body grew from four hundred members to several thousand. Each Lord's Day, as choruses of hymns and praise were being sung by the rest of the congregation, individuals would stand to their feet and confess their sins out loud. The author makes clear that this was not an exercise in over-scrupulosity or in airing one's dirty laundry (most of the confessions couldn't be heard by the singers). It was a necessary act of obedience in confessing one's sins before another. Much of the power to believe during that time of persecution was directly attributed to this liturgical form of confession.

I believe the key to unlocking God's great power in any church is corporate confession. James 5:16 reads, "Therefore confess your sins to each other and pray for one other so that you may be healed." How we need spiritual healing in our day; and I am learning that healing—of mind and body and soul—is most often accomplished in a climate of holiness, in an atmosphere where "the prayer of a righteous man has great power in its effects." And yet, I cannot coordinate the "corporate bathing" of the church. I am not in a position of power and influence like that of Hezekiah, the Jewish King who commanded the priests, "Listen to me, Levites! Consecrate yourselves now and consecrate the temple of the LORD, the God of your fathers. Remove all defilement from the sanctuary" (2 Chronicles 29:5).

But I am responsible for the cleanliness of the interior temple of my own being. There are several lavers at which I can bathe. There is the private confessional which I practice in daily prayer. This begins with a soul-check which inquires, "Lord, have I erred in any way today? Show me my transgression. Hear my confession, forgive, and cleanse." This discipline is one of the differences between a mature or an immature Christian life.

Confession must also be practiced at the corporate laver—between individuals. If I have openly abused a fellow Christian, if I have overtly brought grief into another life, then I must go about the work of repentance and restitution in order to restore that relationship. I must find the courage to say, "I have been wrong. Forgive me my errors."

There is also the laver of going to a trusted spiritual advisor and confessing those errors we have confessed in private but for which we have found no release. This rite is an ancient and powerful form misunderstood either through neglect or through casual overuse. W. Ross Foley in *You Can Win Over Weariness* quotes O. Hobart Mowrer, a psychologist:

> I am persuaded that healing and redemption depend much more upon what we say about ourselves to others, significant others, than upon what others (no matter how highly trained or untrained, ordained or unordained) say to us. It's the truth we ourselves speak, rather than the treatment we receive, that heals us.[2]

Then Mr. Foley goes on to say that "Confession that breaks the shroud of our secrecy and leads us out into the open before God and a group of significant other people will liberate us from fear and guilt in a way that nothing else can."[3]

I remember an incident of going to the laver of open confession. I had been experiencing one of those times when reading Scripture tasted like an exercise in eating ashes; my prayers were all grounded soon after takeoff, and God seemed far away. I had confessed my errors privately to the Lord, but there had been no restoration of my soul. I had confessed the coldness of my heart to family and close friends. I had invited their prayers of concern, but still I plodded through this spiritual desert.

And then one Sunday morning our pastor left a little time at the end of his sermon for people to openly express their feelings to the Lord. It was just a few minutes, but I grabbed them to utter my timid prayer, "Lord, I confess to you before this congregation that I have lost my first love. Restore unto me the joy of my salvation." This was no big production. There were other prayers being prayed. Mine was just one slipped among the many—but it was an open prayer of confession.

The heavens opened. Rain came. I became ravenous once again for the spiritual disciplines. Intimacy with God returned. Joy bounded like a wild gazelle in my soul.

David and I are now attending a church where, for the first time in my Christian life, I am able to avail myself of this rite of confession in the presence of a trusted spiritual director. I have found its powerful efficacy (although used only on rare occasions) to be like a fireman's hose flushing out the accumulated junk of my inner life.

Have you washed your hands today?

Psalm 26 is a song of the child who has washed. "I do not sit with deceitful men, nor do I consort with hypocrites; I abhor the assembly of evildoers and refuse to sit with the wicked. I wash my hands in innocence, and go about your altar, O LORD, proclaiming aloud your praise and telling of all your wonderful deeds" (4-7).

You can sing again. You can climb the hill to his great house. You can sit at your Papa's table. You can wear the festal garments with the seal that proclaims you an heir. Just listen to your Father's voice. He's simply saying what every good parent who loves his child always says. "Have you washed your hands? Good. Come and dine."

How could any of us want to be anything but clean?

The Prayer for Washing

Lord,
I have discovered that I am filthy.
I have not scrubbed enough.
I have not washed thoroughly.
I come before you for cleansing.

Dear Papa,
I confess my dirtiness.
I pray for forgiveness.

Wash me—my hands, my face,
My most hidden inner self.
Make me clean.
Wrap me in the wooly towel of your love.
Let me sit at your table today,
I pray.
Amen.

1. F. Kefa Sampangi, *A Distant Grief* (Glendale, Calif.: Regal Books, 1979).
2. W. Ross Foley, *You Can Win over Weariness* (Glendale, Calif.: Regal Books, 1977), p. 127.
3. Ibid., p. 128.

The Discipline of Inner Cleansing

Suggested passages for study and meditation: Psalm 15; Psalm 32:1-6; Psalm 51; 1 John 1:5-9; James 5:16

Hymns for meditation: "Jesus, Lover of My Soul"
"There Is a Fountain"
"Rock of Ages"
"Nothing But the Blood"

I believe God is wanting to teach me more about inner cleansing because:

This concept is not new; I have previously learned something about confession when:

The Scripture(s) God is impressing upon my heart that underscores this discipline is written out below.

What this Scripture means in terms of my personal situation is:

Other incidents have come to bear on my learning process: I have read something in a book; a friend spoke a pertinent word; my memory was jogged about an almost forgotten event. Such additional experiences are:

As an indication of my intent to develop this inner discipline, I will pray "The Prayer for Washing." I have prayed the prayer (circle the appropriate numbers):

Seven days, twice a day

1 2 3 4 5 6 7 8 9 10 11 12 13 14

Thirty days, once a day

1 2 3 4 5 6 7 8 9 10 11 12 13 14

15 16 17 18 19 20 21 22 23 24 25 26 27 28 29 30

During the above learning time frame, the friend I will share this learning process with is:

2

KEEPIN' TALKIN':

The Discipline of Constantly Communicating with God

When our eldest son was small, my husband and I set up a homegrown recording studio in order to tape the adorable phrases, songs, and sayings which we were sure indicated genius in our child. The supper dishes had been cleared away and David brought out his tape recorder; we established ourselves at the dining room table with child at hand.

With technology in place—the borrowed Wallensack reel-to-reel recorder winding round and round—the only difficulty that presented itself was our bright offspring's refusal to cooperate. Beyond responding (very softly and most recalcitrantly) to "How does the cow go?" and "What does the horsie say?" Randy was deliberately mute. No rapid flow of sing-song baby rhymes, no darling, mispronounced Sunday school songs. Much to our exasperation, there was nothing—and the tape rolled on and on, capturing only the pleas and cajolements of us, the parents.

Finally, we resorted to threats. The most hated activity above all hated activities was "beddy-bye time." When Randy refused to cooperate (and with the tape recorder still rolling) we would sternly announce, "Okay. It's beddy-bye time." Instantly, this adamantly silent two-year-old became the world's model child, "I keepin' talkin'," he pattered. "I keepin' talkin'."

Then after a flow of phrases—itsy-bitsy spider, Jesus loves me, six little ducks that I once knew—his interest would lag. We would repeat *beddy-bye time* with more than a hint of threat, and he would wind up his vocal gymnastics again with "I keepin' talkin', I keepin' talkin'."

Our machinations continued until we had wrangled from him one full side of a tape of sounds.

"Keepin' talkin'" has become an important hallmark of our relationship with all four of our children. "Mom, Dad, can I talk to you?" is a signal David and I try to heed at bedtime, after school, and especially at the inevitably inconvenient hours—right before company arrives, as we're frantically making preparations to fly out of town, or when we're all talked out ourselves after days of conferences, planning meetings, and brainstorm sessions. I believe that as long as we can keep the communication channels open, there is hope for overcoming all difficulties. We do not accept such defeated expressions as, "I don't want to talk about it" or "I don't know" or non-verbal shrugs, grimaces, or downcast eyes.

Through these years of marriage, David and I have also had to "keepin' talkin'. " As with any married couple, we have had difficulties for which we both felt no solutions could be found. Eventually, after much marital trial and error, we discovered that if we can just talk the problem out . . . if we can exhaust all the possibilities by earnest discussion . . . if we can give to and receive from one another a fair hearing . . . if we can ask enough defining questions to force clear and concise expression, then often the best of solutions finally comes.

Admittedly, the resolutions to certain problems seemed to take forever. I remember thinking about one, *We're going to keep talking about this for the rest of our married lives. We'll be infirm, decrepit, in a nursing home—and still be talking. I think it will eventually bore me to tears.* But we hadn't been totally honest with each other. Once we finally had courage to discover and reveal our true feelings, the long-delayed resolutions came hurrying after. Through this particular log jam in the river of our love, I learned that while "keepin' talkin'," it is important to be honest.

When human relationships break down, when there is alienation, it is often impossible to communicate. Sometimes we need to take a breather from one another, or circumstances force us to do so. But as a general rule of thumb, whenever even the slightest opportunity offers itself for re-establishing communication—even if it is at the most mundane level—we must grab the frail opportunity. Write a letter. Make a phone call. Talk about the weather, the children, the day's activities.

You can't "keepin' talkin'" if you're not talking at all.

For years, February days when I was housebound with small children were the hardest times of all; the climatic effect rolling off Lake Michigan bogged down northern Illinois with clubfooted weather. I longed for the sun to shine two successive days in a row. I yearned for spring, knowing all too well that madding March with its melted layers of accreted winter's filth barred my isolated heart from the rioting green blooms of April. It was during these shadowy days, dragging with plodding prisoner's feet, that I learned how important it is to "keepin' talkin'" with God.

A major part of the mature Christian journey is learning how to handle those times when the heavens are locked, when our lives are weighted with the winter garments of despair, pain, worry, and loss. We try desperately to convince ourselves that we don't serve a God who has absented himself from the listening post, who has not hung up a "Shop's Closed" sign and taken off to vacation somewhere in the balmy south.

The Psalms are a prayer journal, an ongoing record of one man's conversations with God. Many of these poem-songs are about times when David hit a roadblock to intimate dialogue with God:

> O LORD, how many are my foes! How many rise up against me! Many are saying of me, "God will not deliver him" (3:1)
>
> Give ear to my words, O LORD, consider my sighing. Listen to my cry for help, my King and my God (5:1-2b).
>
> O LORD, do not rebuke me in your anger or discipline me in your wrath. Be merciful to me, LORD, for I am faint; O LORD, heal me, for my bones are in agony (6:1-2).

David's words reiterate the old truth I began to learn while sitting at the dining table, tutored by my own small child: When your soul feels like a gray February day, and all seems to be rain, fog, and chill drizzle, the overcast can be lifted if you will learn to just "keepin' talkin'" with God.

David was so utterly honest in his feelings toward the Lord. He vented his frustration. He named his insecurities. He cataloged his fears. The Psalms contain none of the macho-tough "strong-men-aren't-weepy" stuff. There is none of this misguided piety which often characterizes the twentieth-century Christian. Divinity doesn't have to be protected from blasts of honesty, from muddy doubts, and from half-frozen ponds of winter emotions. David was wise enough in his knowledge of Yahweh to know that when the Februarys of life were pinching the emotions, God was already aware of the fact; so he just "kept talkin'" and made sure that the feelings he expressed were as honest and as truthful as possible.

"Why, O LORD, do you stand far off? Why do you hide yourself in times of trouble?" In other words, "Where are you God when I need you? Why aren't you behaving on my behalf like you promised to behave?" These are prayers of ventilation for our inner selves, like windows open on stuffy bedrooms that air the linen, the carpets, and the lace curtains with fresh air in exchange for the de-oxygenated atmosphere of closed rooms.

Through the years, the honest sessions between myself and my God have become so beneficial that I often recommend them to people who come to me for help. "Have you told God how you feel?" I will ask.

No, she's been afraid to express her anger to God. She preferred not to tell the Awesome One she felt he had abandoned her. And I often laugh when I hear comments like this. Even as the words were uttered in human confidentiality, God overheard the conversation! Even before our talk, God knew what my friend was feeling. I usually encourage a ventilation session with God, and almost without exception my friend reports to me that this honest, sometimes vehement exchange of negative emotions and ideas clears the air between herself and her Creator. "I feel so much better," she will say. Invariably she expresses how overwhelmed she is with a God who loves her enough to allow her to be utterly honest with him.

"Keepin' talkin'" is a way of airing our souls of the ideas and concepts that have kept us from experiencing God's care; often, after ventilation, we are aired enough to experience more of his surprising love for us. We must learn not to stop talking when our hearts are overburdened, when our prayers go unanswered, when it seems as though our spiritual siblings always get a hearing and we don't—then more than ever, don't stop talking.

God is listening. In one sense, he is always communing. It is we ourselves who are inept at honest communication with our Heavenly Parent. It only *seems* as though he's silent; many times he's waiting for us to "keepin' talkin'" so that we can finally become honest.

Perhaps your soul has been in the middle of a February day that seems to be lasting longer than any February day should. Go to the Psalms. Take paper and pencil and jot down the amazing range of emotions David expressed—anger, joy, confidence.

Keepin' Talkin'

As you read each psalm, note especially how it ends. There is rarely a February day psalm that doesn't end with a rapture of praise and trust. Psalm 7, for example, begins with, "O LORD my God, I take refuge in you" and goes on to record David's fear and terror as he helplessly faces evil pursuers. It ends with, "I will give thanks to the LORD because of his righteousness and will sing praise to the name of the LORD Most High." See if you can draw some application to your own circumstances from the conclusions David draws regarding his God.

Then write out your own February day prayer. Begin it by saying:

> Lord, today feels like a February day in my soul. But I want to "keepin' talkin'." I don't want communication to shut down between us because of this despair, this depression, this gloom. I want to tell you exactly how I feel—

Continue to communicate until you have reached that point where you know you are no longer hiding anything from him or anything from yourself. At this point, the surprising inward prayer dialogue begins again; now your words are no longer a one-way communication battering frantically heavenward, but they become a two-way exchange with God's marvelous, soothing love beginning to expand in your aired-out soul.

Once the windows to the soul have been opened—and once the frustrations, the frights, the human frailties have been aired—then the soul gazes godward, light breaks the gloom, the clouds part; we see him. We know with whom we are speaking.

The Keepin' Talkin' Prayer

Lord,
I promise that to the best of my ability
I will keep talking with you.

I will not let hurts, disappointments, fatigue
or general wretchedness cut me off in communicating
my feelings to you.

Help me to be honest, and help me always to understand that
though there are times I stop talking with you, there are never
times when you stop talking to me.
Amen.

The Discipline of Constantly Communicating with God

Suggested passages for study and meditation: Hebrews 4:14-16, 5:7; 2 Peter 2:4-10. Read through the Psalms and write down the range of emotions David experienced. How honest was he in his expressions to God? Note how each psalm ends—what can you learn from this?

Hymns for meditation: "Nothing Between"
"I Need Thee Every Hour"
"No One Understands Like Jesus"
"What a Friend We Have in Jesus"

I believe God wants to teach me more about constantly communing with him because:

This concept is not new; I previously learned something about my need to continually be talking with God when:

The Scripture(s) God is impressing upon my heart that underscores this discipline is written out below.

What this Scripture means in terms of my personal situation is:

Other incidents have come to bear on my learning process: I have read something in a book; a friend spoke a pertinent word; my memory was jogged about an almost forgotten event. Such additional experiences are:

As an indication of my intent to develop this inner discipline, I will pray "The Keepin' Talkin' Prayer." I have prayed the prayer

(circle the appropriate numbers):

Seven days, twice a day

1 2 3 4 5 6 7 8 9 10 11 12 13 14

Thirty days, once a day

1 2 3 4 5 6 7 8 9 10 11 12 13 14

15 16 17 18 19 20 21 22 23 24 25 26 27 28 29 30

During the above learning time frame, the friend I will share this learning process with is:

3

A LIVING ICON:

The Discipline of Looking Up

Dancing on My Grave, an autobiography of prima ballerina Gelsey Kirkland, focuses on Kirkland's rise in the high-pressure world of ballet, on her relationship with such ballet greats as Ballanchine, Baryshnikov, Peter Martin, and on her eventual decline into illness, drug addiction, and suicidal despair.

A particularly revealing passage describes the relationship between the dancer and the mirror in the practice studio. Ms. Kirkland writes:

> The relationship between the dancer and her mirror image is an intimacy of extraordinary power and potentially perilous consequence.
>
> As a primary teaching tool for dance, the mirror fosters the delusion that beauty is only skin-deep, that truth is found only in the plasticity of movement. It seems preferable to imitate rather than create. Imitation can be varied to create the impression of originality. . . .
>
> The dancer is trained to watch, to enter the world of the mirror until it is no longer necessary to even look. To the extent that a dancer becomes a complacent reflection, he or she does not learn to test beauty or to discover its inner life. In this way, the mirror can trap a dancer's soul, ultimately breaking the creative spirit. Such a dancer is created, but does not know how to create. With success and popularity, the situation becomes more precarious. At any moment, with the capricious changes of fashion, a glance to check the mirror may reveal tragedy—that he or she has been created for nothing.[1]

Much of the rest of the book shows how that nothingness eventually engulfed Gelsey Kirkland in its wide jaws of destruction. But in truth, the mirror image, or some form of it, is what leads the average person—the person with no claims to artistic achievement or fame—to downfall as well. Frankly, we often cannot stop looking at ourselves. This perverse tendency, at its worst, has entered into our cultural understanding through the psychological term *narcissism*, an excessive interest in one's own appearance, comfort, or importance.

This word is derived from Greek mythology—a tale of the handsome youth, Narcissus, who was very proud of his own beauty. Many young women loved him, but he paid no attention to them. One, Echo, was so hurt by his coldness that all but her voice faded away. The gods were angered by this, and they punished Narcissus by making him fall in love with his own reflection in a pool of clear water. He was so much in love with himself that he could not leave the pool and at last he died.

I've counseled with some people so caught up in watching themselves that when I describe them in the following way, they immediately agree that my description is uncannily accurate. I say to them, "You are like a vulture sitting on a wire fence watching every word and thought and act that you yourself speak, think, or do. You cock your vulture's head, you peer, you wait to pounce; you pounce, and then you tear apart, you shred, you bloody your own inner self."

Self-focus which borders on fixation is always an invitation to death of some sort—a decline in the quality of our human relationships or the increased possibility of emotional maladjustment. Self-fixation is always a symptom of spiritual maladjustment, childishness; moreover, the very act of gazing at ourselves often prohibits spiritual growth.

And life, life is filled with crises—the inconvenient as well as the catastrophic. Crises, more than anything, focus our attention on ourselves. We focus on our pain, on our discomfort, on our financial distress, on the way our children's misbehavior has embarrassed us, on the neglect of our spouse, on our own hurt. Like Gelsey Kirkland, we find ourselves doing daily exercises in front of the practice mirror with each session capturing more of our soul, while unknowingly we become a complacent reflection of our own selves. Like Narcissus, we gaze into the pool of water, developing a habit of self-watching which threatens to become addictive the more we gaze, robbing us of our creative powers for growth.

The only cure for this debilitating habit of self-gazing is to refocus our gaze, to cast it away from the mirror—outward and preferably upward. Hebrews 12:1-2 exhorts us to do just this, "Let us throw off everything that hinders and the sin that so easily entangles, and let us run with perseverance the race marked out for us. Let us fix our eyes on Jesus, the author and perfecter of our faith. . . ."

Admittedly, this upward sight is difficult to establish. We're often like those Greeks who came to Philip and said to him, "Sir, we wish to see Jesus." The inclination of our heart is to cast our gaze toward him, to be freed from the dancerlike preoccupation with our own mirror image. We believe John's promise recorded in 1 John 3:2, "Dear friends, now we are children of God, and what we will be has not yet been made known. But we know that when he appears, we shall be like him, for we shall see him as he is."

How do we *see* Jesus?

How do we shift our gaze from the parallel bar to the perpendicular cross? How do we develop the habit of looking upward instead of inward? How in the midst of crisis and pain do we look to him instead of to ourselves?

The best way for us to develop this discipline is to deliberately look upward for a little bit each day. We focus on the scriptural record of the life of Christ. We read about him and we think about what we have read. We ask the Holy Spirit to teach us what he is like. We wake in the morning and before we jump out of bed, we pray a prayer of gratitude to him. We mark down, in a prayer journal, on a sheet slipped into our Bible: *I have lifted my eyes today. I have thought about Christ.* By these small means and others, in increments, often without emotion, our gaze is lifted. We lift our eyes to Christ day after day after day after day.

Dr. Maxwell Maltz, the author of *Psycho-Cybernetics*, wrote that regardless of a person's age or sex, it takes twenty-one days to change a habit. Through his work as a plastic surgeon, Maltz discovered that in virtually every case involving amputation it took his patient twenty-one days to lose the ghost-image of the missing limb. Maltz began to study the correlation between the human mind and the twenty-one-day period. He proved scientifically that an idea must be repeated for twenty-one days before it becomes permanently fixed in the subjective, motivating mind.

There are fifty-two weeks in a year, 365 days; that is seventeen discipline-improving segments. The Christian woman who develops the habit of looking to Christ day after day will be freed from the destructive tendency of gazing into the mirror-image of herself. She will no longer be a pale imitation of her own image; she will begin "becoming like him, seeing him as he is."

A discipline is often difficult to establish if we don't keep the end result in mind. The end result is not only freedom from the fixated focus on ourselves; it is also the ability to free others from their own mirror gaze.

Let me illustrate.

I often find myself in unusual circumstances. One of these was a visit to the bombed-out city of Beirut, the once beautiful capital city of Lebanon. I've seen the frequent results of power politics—the refugees in camps, their despair, malnourishment, deprivation; I've heard the sound of mortars firing over borders; I've been driven through military check-points; I've interviewed innocent victims as they fled for their lives. But before my visit to Beirut, I had never actually been in a war zone. Consequently, the city stands out in my memory.

The small group with which I was traveling was taken into the hills above the city to the University of the Holy Spirit, an institute of higher learning that managed to continue the business of academia despite the conflict tearing the country apart. It was run by monks of the Maronite order, a branch of the Eastern Christian church.

I'll never forget vespers that evening. One hundred and fifty monks in their black cassocks gathered for evensong, and the whole liturgical service was sung in a language of Aramaic derivation. The voices of the men, full-bodied, robust, accompanied by flute and a stringed instrument, filled the plain chapel. And although I couldn't understand the words, their melodic praises filled my heart. I was euphoric with worship by the time we left to gather in the large hall for dinner.

Huge murals adorned each wall at the ends of the room, impressionistic paintings of Christ feeding the five thousand, of Christ calling the disciples. By chance, my dinner companion was the art director of the university, and we began to discuss art. When I asked him in what field of art he specialized, he replied, "Icons."

"Icons?" (I thought icons had gone out with the last of the Romanoffs.)

"Oh, yes," he said, smiling at my ignorance. "I paint contemporary icons. Would you like to see my icons?"

Could there have been any circumstance more unusual?—an evangelical pastor's wife amongst the monks of the University of the Holy Spirit, one of a few women dining in a hall filled with men, most of whom couldn't speak my language. Above the war-torn city of Beirut, I was being asked by a heretofore stranger if I would like to see his icons.

But I am also ever for adventure, so we went down to the art studio where I received my first lecture on icons. "You see," said my new friend, "most Westerners think that the style of icons—where dimension is flat, where there's no perspective to draw the eye of the viewer into the painting—was popular because the religious art of the early centuries had not developed a two- or three-dimensional capability."

"Oh, no?" said I, that having been exactly my thought.

"No," said he. "The flatness is intentional. The artist drew about religious subjects, often for people who couldn't read (these paintings were their books); but he drew in such a way intentionally, so that the eye of the viewer was drawn, not into the painting, but hopefully upward toward God."

I think about Beirut each time I hear about another car bombing, or about fighting across the "green line," or of terrorists who take hostages, and I think about Christians such as those who have understanding in areas of faith where I have only prejudices and ignorance. I think about that monk painting contemporary icons in a warring country in the hopes that his paintings will refract the gaze of the viewer Godward.

And I think: In this warring world, I want to be a Living Icon. I want the gaze of those who view me to be refracted upward. I don't want others to be captured with the dimension of my life. Too much attention focused on me is bound to reveal imperfections in the human work. I want them to see on me the reflection of the multi-dimensional image of my perfect Creator.

Who of us hasn't had the experience of going along with a large crowd, perhaps at a fairground, perhaps in a city? One person spots something unusual in the sky or on a tall building or on a flag pole. He strains his neck, he peers into the upward distance and soon numbers have stopped their hurrying steps; they too are looking up, straining to see, pointing at the unusual sight.

I cannot be a Living Icon, refracting the gaze of others from me to him, if I don't look upward myself.

To be free to look upward is why many have taken the vow of poverty, why many have dispossessed themselves of lands and businesses and homes. If my sight becomes filled with what I own, my head will be pulled parallel, maybe even cast down. Saints have always known this: *Whatever I possess possesses me*. So they have held lightly all material things. But the gaze at the mirror-image is a different matter altogether. We cannot give away ourselves when our selves are always with us. There is one cure for this fixated focus: to glance determinedly at Christ.

The Psalmist understood that whatever we turn our gaze to fills our vision. Psalm 123 says, "I lift up my eyes to you. . . . As the eyes of slaves look to the hand of their master, as the eyes of a maid look to the hand of her mistress, so our eyes look to the LORD our God." We must make Christ the Possessor. Like Paul, we must learn to allow him to possess us so that our gaze will be filled with him. In Philippians 3:12, 14 Paul says, "I press on to take hold of that for which Christ Jesus took hold of me. . . . to win the prize for which God has called me heavenward in Christ Jesus."

I am determined to free myself from the mirror-image. I am determined, in this warring world, to be a Living Icon. I'm getting ready for that coming day when we all stand in a crowd, looking up.

1. Gelsey Kirkland, *Dancing on My Grave* (New York: Doubleday, 1986), p. 73.

The Prayer for Looking Up

Lord,
Give me the grace to look up,
to be freed from my own image,
from my own mirror-reflection.
Loosen the hold upon me
of many possessions.
Help me to lift my head
and see you.
Fill my vision, I pray.
Amen.

THE DISCIPLINE OF LOOKING UP

Suggested passages for study and meditation: Psalm 123; Philippians 3:12-21; Hebrews 3:1 and Hebrews 12:2. In order to keep your eyes more consciously on Christ, read through a gospel account this month. As you read, write down qualities in Christ that need to be perfected in you. Ask yourself, How can I be a reflection of Christ today?

Hymns for meditation: "My Desire"
"O to Be Like Thee"
"May the Mind of Christ My Savior"
"O, For a Thousand Tongues to Sing"

I believe God is wanting to teach me more about gazing Godward because:

This concept is not new; I have previously learned something about keeping my focus on Christ when:

The Scripture(s) God is impressing upon my heart that underscores this discipline is written out below.

What this Scripture means in terms of my personal situation is:

Other incidents have come to bear on my learning process: I have read something in a book; a friend spoke a pertinent word; my memory was jogged about an almost forgotten event. Such additional experiences are:

As an indication of my intent to develop this inner discipline, I will pray "The Prayer for Looking Up." I have prayed the prayer

(circle the appropriate numbers):

Seven days, twice a day

1 2 3 4 5 6 7 8 9 10 11 12 13 14

Thirty days, once a day

1 2 3 4 5 6 7 8 9 10 11 12 13 14

15 16 17 18 19 20 21 22 23 24 25 26 27 28 29 30

During the above learning time frame, the friend I will share this learning process with is:

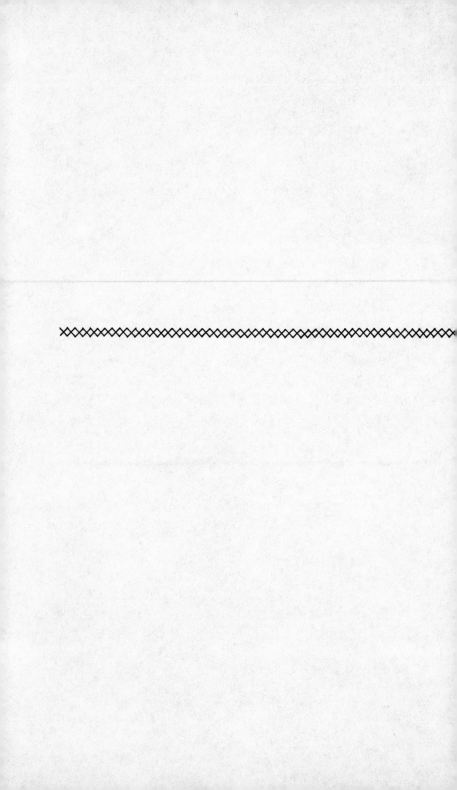

4

GREETING THE DAY:

The Discipline of Celebrating New Moments

While traveling in Kenya in the east horn of Africa, my companions and I spent a night high in the mountains in a settlement called Gatab. Like many missionary aviation runways, the one at Gatab had been carved out of a flat edge of the mountain. As our little plane coasted to a stop, I estimated that we were landing perilously close to the precipice, which jutted over a multiple thousand foot drop.

"What happens if you don't stop in time?" I called from the back of the plane as the pilot worked the brakes and the controls.

"You fall off," he replied nonchalantly, veering the plane around, the wings tilting with the edge of air above the abrupt incline. He proceeded to taxi back to the anchoring post where the vehicle was finally secured against crosscurrents and unpredictable mountain winds.

Much of the dinner table discussion of that evening, around kerosene lamplight, centered on near misses while flying in and out of Gatab.

The next morning, rising before the rest of the household had awakened, I dressed in the half-light and slipped out along the mountain path, edged by mid-height grasses still bent heavy with their morning load of dew. I went out to examine the sheer two thousand foot drop for myself. We had made it safely in without my help; could we make it safely away without it?

By nature I am a morning person and I reveled in this particular day-tome, this book left casually open for my eyes to read. Woven stick fences lined the clay-red path leading to compounds where families lived out lives unfamiliar to me. But the local inhabitants were morning risers, day greeters. Small fires blew smoky notice to the lifting sun. Boys, barefoot, skinny, and chilled in this mountain air, herded goats and cattle with slender stick cudgels. Atonal cow bells began the morning chant—*abahabah.* The boys stared at me wide-eyed, wondering at my walking presence. Men about their duties smiled and I smiled in return, the only language we knew to speak what was near our hearts, "Good day to you. Good new day."

I treaded the runway, my sandals soaked, to the very edge of the precipice; I sat wedged on its rim, my legs braced against firm, adamantine boulders, ancient old rocks birthed in this middle womb of the world. My heart flew up with the soaring birds overhead. I watched them cast off, out over the canyon, drop and rise, drop and rise effortlessly, joy in their cry and joy in my muted human echo. I had brought my Bible and a copy of A. W. Tozer's *The Knowledge of the Holy.* And there at Gatab, with horizons of hills rolling away one beyond the other and breasting the valley far beneath me, while watching the birds' exultant floating—there, tears came. I read the Psalms blinking and then breakfasted upon profound praise from Tozer. And I exalted the great glorious beauty, calling greeting to the One who is God of the day, Lord of all mornings. Hail Thou!

I have always been a morning person. Patterned in the pre-birth world by a morning mother, I wake early, before light, and lie with the morning thought, *Ah, life again!* Even as a child I greeted the day thus from earliest memory—again, again, again.

Unfortunately, I grow impatient with any in my family who wish to sleep beyond seven. David teases me about bouncing out of bed, instantly awake, alive—no yawning, no stretching, no coming to terms gently with daybreak. I'm impatient to get going at four o'clock! A perfect morning is waking while it is dark with hours before light—doing housework, desk organization, having morning prayer. Then I hurry off to walk/run my three-and-a-half miles before the sun has risen high enough to burn off the mist on the Illinois fields or to dissipate the fog that lies in the dip of the road along which I go.

It has always been easier for me to pray at the beginning of the day rather than at day's end. By night I'm fatigued, folding inward, mellowing. I can organize my thoughts better, and capture the will-o'-the-wisp lambent lyrics of writing in natural light where ideas are not mediated by an artificial bulb, ("100 watts average during life; or 3-way lite, initial 51/153/204"). For years when I was a young mother, these were my precious few hours of peak energy. I learned to use them to maximum efficiency; by noon I was starting to sag.

I remember habitually reading to my sleeping children portions of a poem I have paperclipped in one of my notebooks. "The way to start a day is this: Go outside and face the east and greet the sun with some kind of blessing, or chant a song that you made yourself and keep for early mornings."

A new day needs to be honored. Primitive peoples the world over have always known that a new day is sacred, a gift of the gods perhaps not to be repeated tomorrow. They sensed that a new day needed help in rising, so they sang and wafted smoke and sent flowers along on streams. They drummed sunrise songs in the Congo and leaped to Aztec flutes in Mexico. They rang a thousand small bells in China. Some sent good thoughts to the day, some floated feathers on the four winds. They faced the east with prayer papers and waited breathless to watch if the new day would come one more time; and they welcomed it when it broke the horizon, bleeding roseate stains across the sky. And they watched the sun carry fire and light and held up their babies to behold it. And their hearts were grateful for one more, a new day in which to live.

I agree, that's the way to start a day.

And we, we of the Christianized, technological, intellectually superior, modern world? We slap off the jangling alarm, roll over in bed, groan, yawn, bury our head beneath our pillows and scarcely realize the sacred moment of praise is passing. A moment we will never have again, never hold to our heart—not this way, not *this* moment.

Most of us have forgotten how to greet the day. The knowledge is all but lost to us that a new day is sacred: a gift from God, a rare and precious gift. A new day brings with it another opportunity to start all over, to raise one's head from the pillow with a glad heart, to watch the clouds roll across the dark sky now diffusing pink, and to breathe that child prayer of gratitude, "Oh, God, life again. Again, one more day of life."

We must relearn how to stand in awe, how to face for a moment the eastern sky with praise and thanksgiving and allow our hearts to be filled with a corresponding inner daybreak of adoration.

We must learn to not ever take for granted—no matter how pain-filled our life—that we are alive and the earth still turns on its axis, that evil has not wobbled the world off its course while we slept; and we must understand this sacramental symbol, this reenactment of life which comes resurrecting every twenty-four hours.

Celebrating each new day helps us develop the ability to be grateful for all new moments and for the God who is in each one. The discipline of celebrating each new day influences our attitude toward all of life.

A new day signifies: The Lord of mornings is still sovereign over the world.

In response we sing:

> The heavens declare the glory of God;
>   the skies proclaim the work of his hands.
> Day after day they pour forth speech;
>   night after night they display knowledge.
> In the heavens he has pitched a tent
>   for the sun, which is like a bridegroom
>   coming forth from his pavilion,
>   like a champion rejoicing to run his course.
> It rises at one end of the heavens
>   and makes its circuit to the other;
>   nothing is hidden from its heat (Psalm 19:1-2,
>   4b-6).

Nature shouts of this beginning-again-God, this God who can make all our failures regenerative, the One who is God of risings again, who never tires of fresh starts, nativities, or renaissances in persons or in cultures. God is a God of starting over, of genesis and regenesis. He composts life's sour fruits, moldering rank and decomposing; he applies the organic matter to our new day chances; he freshens the world with dew; he hydrates withered human hearts with his downpouring Spirit.

Joy fills me on these first-thought mornings. I'm eager to hear God speak to me, to begin the inner dialogue this new day affords. It's easy to offer myself up, to say, "What do you want me to do for you today? Here am I, Lord; use me as you please." And then without even getting out of bed, intercession comes. I can naturally spend that first hour of the day in prayer with my Lord on the mornings when my first thoughts are of him. I pray for the protection and wholeness of my children. I pray for strength for my husband and help for him as he does his work. On and on the prayers go.

When I am aware of Christ in my new day (and in the middle of my wakeful nights), then I am able to receive all things from his hand. The classic prayer of St. Francis de Sales becomes my own—"Yes, God, Yes, and always Yes!" I can accept not only the potentiality of beauty in this gift of a new day; I can also accept the pain, the disappointment, the disaster.

Nor do I ever want to cry, "Just one more day, Lord. Just one more day." I don't want to ever regret that I didn't live the gift of days completely, with my whole heart, my face lifted to the light. He has measured our moments, allotted our span of time. I want only to appreciate fully what he has chosen for me—this day now, now, now.

A New Day Prayer

Oh, Lord,
Help me to hold this moment to my heart,
this new day.

Help me to see it as a rare gift of promise,
filled with the potential of living life well,
of remaking old ways new,
of saying Yes to each opportunity, large and small,
of saying Yes to you.

Help me to begin each new day with you in my thoughts,
my first thoughts.

And let me be glad that I have these hours of life to live.
Help me to live them well—now.
Amen.

The Discipline of Celebrating New Moments

Suggested passages for study and meditation: Jesus' example—Mark 1:35; Psalm 5:1-3; Psalm 57:7-11; Psalm 108:1-5; Psalm 63; Psalm 100:1-4; Isaiah 26:9

Hymns for meditation: "Holy, Holy, Holy"
"Great Is Thy Faithfulness"
"May Jesus Christ Be Praised"
"Awake, My Soul"

I believe God wants to teach me more about having my first thoughts fly to him because:

This concept is not new; I have previously learned something about this discipline when:

The Scripture(s) God is impressing upon my heart that underscores this discipline is written out below.

Greeting the Day

What this Scripture means in terms of my personal situation is:

Other incidents have come to bear on my learning process: I have read something in a book; a friend spoke a pertinent word; my memory was jogged about an almost forgotten event. Such additional experiences are:

As an indication of my intent to develop this inner discipline, I will pray "A New Day Prayer." I have prayed the prayer (circle the appropriate numbers):

Seven days, twice a day

1 2 3 4 5 6 7 8 9 10 11 12 13 14

Thirty days, once a day

1 2 3 4 5 6 7 8 9 10 11 12 13 14

15 16 17 18 19 20 21 22 23 24 25 26 27 28 29 30

During the above learning time frame, the friend I will share this learning process with is:

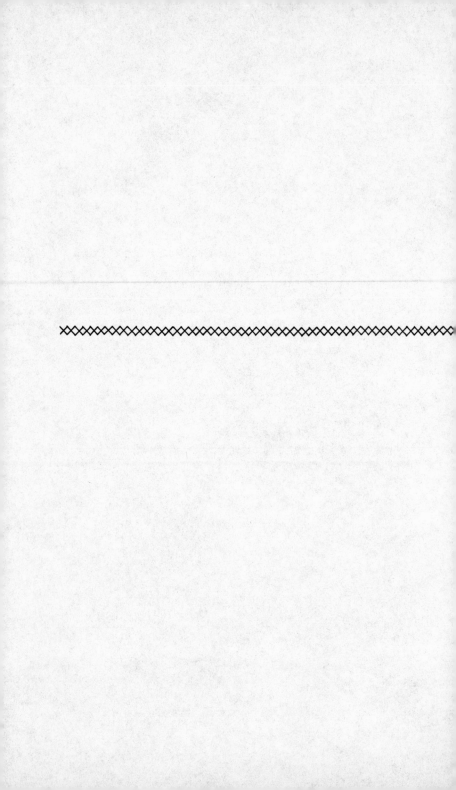

5

THE PARTY WHERE NOBODY CAME:

The Discipline of Gratitude for Disappointments

At heart I am a gardener. When my parents were alive, one of the family rituals was the spring planting of the huge garden out at my father's retirement farm. There was nothing so wonderful as the warm sun, the tractor tilling the soil, the broken sticks with stretched twine marking straight rows, the minutiae-knob feel of seeds falling through the palm of one's hand. There was nothing so wonderful as the sound of birds calling over the far pasture and of little children planting a garden in hope of the squash and green beans and peppers and beets, of carrots and lettuce to come.

Fall brought the bounty; earth and rain and sun had done their work: bushels of butterfly squash, delicately white; cucumbers for dill pickles and relish; zucchini and zucchini and more zucchini; tomatoes for filling canning jars with spaghetti sauce and sweet preserves and plump, skinned spheres. Hurrah! Large pumpkins to drag home and set on the porch on our city block, then pumpkin pies and breads and soup for harvest time and holiday.

To grow my own food—to plant and pick, to touch its firm roundness—gives me a feeling of being linked, integrated, with the natural order of things. I become a part of the ancestral activity of man. The crude hoe breaking clods. The sweat beneath the tied headcloth. The bare feet on the stony soil. This feeling of connectedness, of stretching back to primal beginnings, is extremely satisfactory and worth the labor, the strained muscles, the sunburn, the bugbites, the messy kitchen.

When we moved to our present home, however, a vegetable garden was another matter. To my amazement our strip of usually black, loamish Illinois earth was an unworkable clay with an alkaline balance on the extreme end of the soil tester. We have lived here ten years and it has taken me all this time to make the soil workable. Earlier, when one June came creeping nearer and the garden still wasn't in, I finally admitted that I wasn't going to have a garden for another year. And then I sat down and cried.

The next spring rolled around and I found renewed determination in my gardener's heart. I was resolved that the Mains clan was going to have fresh, homegrown vegetables.

But with my mother's death that January and all the details that had unexpectedly come into my life resulting from that family tragedy, I found myself woefully behind on all deadlines. All my production schedules were bumping into each other and racing neck and neck with a family getaway weekend we had planned for the end of May. A simple look at the calendar warned me that a garden was going to have to compete with speaking assignments, broadcasts, mothering responsibilities, and the children's book that was taking me forever to finish.

So I had a bright idea!

I would give a yard party—one of those old-fashioned work days where friends show up with rakes and shovels in hand and spend three hours together in the backyard. My friends could help me dig flower beds, plant a couple of fruit trees, put in the forsythia bushes I wanted to bloom in the woods, and get the roses pruned and fertilized. Working alongside each other, we would plant a garden with the shared advantage of fellowship, a team of people carving out community.

Fifty invitations were printed at a jiffy printers and hand delivered. I joyously organized a menu: a great pot of spring stew savory with the odor of homemade flavors, green crisp salads, big round loaves of black nourishing bread, spicy thick gingerbread with globs of fresh whipped cream, pots of coffee, pitchers of lemonade, and cookies for the children. (Oh, bring the children! They can run and play and catch the fun of working together, and laugh with each other and chase around and sprinkle blessing on the seeds we put in the ground.) I thought about the many who would come and share in labor (and make living bearable in the face of pain); I imagined the conversation and the way our hoeing and digging and cultivating would be at variance with the greatest of life's disappointments—death; and I would strike a symbolic memory in this backyard with these, my friends, a living memorial to life, life again, life burgeoning, life determined, life in weed and flower and seed and pod. And with foretelling, I felt gratefulness at the work these my willing friends would spare me in the days ahead.

Only one couple came.

We had worked in the yard for a half hour when a sudden storm rose and rained us out, leaving me with a gallon of spring stew, uneaten. And that was the end of my good idea.

Looking at the leftover food and the still uncultivated backyard, I thought, *How can fifty people all have legitimate excuses not to help?* There were any one of several attitudes I could adopt. I could become self-pitying: *No one cares for us. I really don't have any friends who are good in a pinch. David and I can help all kinds of people, but ask them to help us and see what happens!*

Then there was the recriminatory attitude, the pointing of the finger, the casting of blame: *Everyone in our society is so busy. People don't care for people any more. Even in the body of Christ there are few who know the meaning of burden bearing. In an affluent world, people hire jobs done, they don't give of themselves sacrificially.*

But in the middle of my rumination, I had another thought, one that rang clear and sound and true. "*The kingdom of heaven is like a king who prepared a wedding banquet for his son. He sent his servants to those who had been invited to the banquet to tell them to come, but they refused to come. Then he sent some more servants and said, 'Tell those who have been invited that I have prepared my dinner: My oxen and fattened cattle have been butchered, and everything is ready. Come to the wedding banquet.' But they paid no attention and went off—one to his field, another to his business. The rest seized his servants, mistreated them and killed them*" (Matthew 22:2-6).

I am discovering that for the Christian, all of life's disappointments are opportunities to glimpse more clearly the heart of God. After I gave the party where nobody came, I thought, *How must God feel to have planned this beautiful celebration called life, and to have invited friends, only to have them complain and gripe or wish he had planned another kind of party?* He's provided a feast, spared no expense for a lavish spread, a banqueting table filled with the most extravagant foods and elegant table settings and lush flowers, only to have his guests stop before the party and gorge themselves at MacDonald's.

How would it feel to plan the incredible drama of redemption, to suffer and die to give access to those to whom you extended invitation; and then to have them turn their backs and stamp their feet and cry and holler and complain and accuse you of not doing enough?

Have you ever given a party where nobody came? Learning to empathize with God in life's small disappointments—the spilled milk, the dented fenders—helps us empathize with him during the moments of major griefs.

A young man sat in our living room sharing the sad story of how he had loved only to have his beloved love another. *This too,* I thought, feeling his deep pain and bitter disappointment, *is what it is like to know the heart of God.* God knows, more than any human, the meaning of unrequited love. He knows the heartbreak of pouring out his unconditional favor only to have his loved ones prostitute themselves after other lowlife suitors, to whistle from the windows of the red-light district to every passerby, to whore and pimp and become exhibitionists in wantonness.

God knows the pain when a beloved is unfaithful.

We grieve over the deformity of a child and spit at God. Have we no idea that he grieves as much as we? It is his creation that has become malformed, his plan of perfection that has been genetically tampered, his seed of life self-contained within each living form that is constantly in danger of destruction.

We are wounded by broken relationships, by the inexplicable iron curtains that hang in heart and soul between peoples, and we scoff at God thinking he is far away, aloof, uncaring. Yet, God is wounded when his children war; nothing grieves the heart of a parent more than sibling jealousies. His grand love scheme for two to stand together against the alienations, the catastrophes, the disasters; his cherished concept of marriage, the becoming of one flesh, is being dismembered by divorce, torn asunder on the rack of infidelity. God hurts when his children don't love the way he intended for us to love.

We are grieved by death, the death of our parents, the death of a closest friend.

What did God feel like when death entered his beautifully created paradise?

What did God feel when his one child—the only human able to live a life exactly as the Father intended—writhed and vomited on that obscene gibbet thrusting defiantly into heaven? Did he not gasp in horror and turn his face when he heard that scream wrenched from the mangled body of his beloved one, "My God! My God! Why have you forsaken me?"

Death is no more a horror to us than it is to him.

Recently, as I've entered deeper and deeper into my understanding of the work and meaning of intercessory prayer, I've often been overwhelmed by tears. The pain of the human predicament leers at me; it often becomes my own; but mostly, I find myself empathetically identified with the heart of God. For a while I hated this weeping in prayer. Then a wise friend said to me, "But Karen, we give Christ our body in which he can mourn over the wounds of the world. For now he has no body but our own." Catherine de Hueck Doherty in *Poustinia* writes: "It's spontaneous as the wind. I just cry. . . . Afterwards I don't know why I cried or what started or stopped it. But I know that it came from God. Something happened in the world that made God cry and he invited me to cry."[1]

I often weep for love in the presence of Christ, when I sense his nearness as I pray. Oh Lord, I plead, what can I do for you? Can I wash your feet like Mary with tears, with perfume? Can I feed you when you are hungry? Can I get you a pillow so you may rest? Can I sit at your feet and pay rapt attention? What can I do? Can I follow wherever you go? Can I bring you money for your ministry? Can I wrap you in burial garments?

I want *to do* for him, and I often hear the answer, a memory out of Scripture, the words of Christ to his disciples in the Garden of Gethsemane, "Watch. Can you not watch with me this one hour?" And through my prayers, sensitized by disappointment, I am beginning to watch over the world with God.

David has traveled a great deal this year, and I have often been lonely. Loneliness can be a true emotional pain that sears the breastbone and invites that old unwelcome companion, self-pity. But I am learning to watch. I take my pain and I use it to understand the pain of those who are truly alone. I thank God for this privilege, this rare gift of being able to share another's agony in empathy so that my prayers will not be superficial, trite, banal, platitudinous. I pray for Luci, for Madeleine, for Mary Lou, for John, for Becky—the widowed, the alienated, the abandoned.

I couldn't pray the way I am beginning to pray now, I couldn't begin to sense the grieving heart of God had I never given a party where nobody came, had I never made a practice of being grateful for the small disappointments in order to be ready for the large—loving and being rejected, losing cherished humans to death, being cast out from the place of belonging.

I am learning to be grateful for life's disappointments.

The Prayer for Disappointments

Oh God,
Thank you for the privilege of learning
to know your heart.

Thank you for the parties where nobody comes,
for the empty beds, the tears of alienation.
Thank you for life's disappointments.

Without them I too would fall asleep in your Gethsemane.
Help me to watch.
Help me to watch with you. Help me to use life's pains
redemptively.

I give you my body as a place for your tears.
It is one thing I can do for you.
Amen.

1. Catherine de Hueck Doherty, *Poustinia,* (Notre dame, Ind.: Ave Maria Press, 1975).

The Discipline of Gratitude for Disappointments

Suggested passages for study and meditation: Luke 14:15-24; 2 Corinthians 1:3-7; Matthew 23:37-39. Spend some time trying to identify with the sufferings of God: Jeremiah 2 Ezekiel 16 and 22; Hosea. (You may find it helpful to read a commentary of these passages.) As you read, ask the Holy Spirit to give you a deeper understanding of the heart of God.

Hymns for meditation: "O Sacred Head Once Wounded"
"Teach Me Thy Way, O Lord"
"No One Understands Like Jesus"
"O Teach Me What It Meaneth"

I believe God is wanting to teach me more about his heart because:

This concept is not new; I previously learned something about disappointments when:

The Scripture(s) God is impressing upon my heart that underscores this discipline is written out below.

What this Scripture means in terms of my personal situation is:

Other incidents have come to bear on my learning process: I have read something in a book; a friend spoke a pertinent word; my memory was jogged about an almost forgotten event. Such additional experiences are:

As an indication of my intent to develop this inner discipline, I will pray "The Prayer for Disappointments." I have prayed the prayer

(circle the appropriate numbers):

Seven days, twice a day

1 2 3 4 5 6 7 8 9 10 11 12 13 14

Thirty days, once a day

1 2 3 4 5 6 7 8 9 10 11 12 13 14

15 16 17 18 19 20 21 22 23 24 25 26 27 28 29 30

During the above learning time frame, the friend I will share this learning process with is:

6

CHRIST BETWEEN US:

The Discipline of Measuring Our Loves

A book crossed my desk titled *Celtic Prayers*, a collection of old prayers originally passed orally from generation to generation in the Outer Hebrides off the coast of Scotland, now gathered in print at the turn of the century. I love the common usage of these prayers: prayers for dressing, prayers for lighting the fire, prayers for traveling. One in particular stimulated a remarkable new inward discipline, a measurement against which I determine whether the loves in my life are in proper alignment—the too-much loves, the not-enough-loves, the impatient loves. The prayer states:

Christ between Us

Be the eye of God betwixt me and each eye,
the purpose of God betwixt me and each purpose,
the hand of God betwixt me and each hand,
the shield of God betwixt me and each shield,
the desire of God betwixt me and each desire,
the bridle of God betwixt me and each bridle,
and no mouth can curse me.

Be the pain of Christ betwixt me and each pain,
the love of Christ betwixt me and each love,
the dearness of Christ betwixt me and each dearness,
the kindness of Christ betwixt me and each kindness,
the wish of Christ betwixt me and each wish,
the will of Christ betwixt me and each will,
and no venom can wound me.

I breathe the words *Christ betwixt thee and me* when I grow impatient with the phone caller who is talking too long, with the difficult personality who is taxing my resources, with the cranky child, with the co-worker whose mind seems so attractive, with the streetperson I encounter. I breathe the prayer, then see the form of Christ between me and the one to whom I am speaking: How would *he* respond to this one? What words would *he* choose? How would *he* touch? What kind of concern would *he* show? Then I do whatever is closest to what I feel Christ would do that I, in my inadequate humanity, am able to do.

Surprisingly, this measurement often acts as a means of liberation rather than a restraint. I sat once beside a friend, one of those co-workers whose mind I admired, and wondered: *Am I developing too much of a feeling for this person? Christ betwixt thee and me,* I prayed. In my imagination I saw Christ sitting between us; but to my surprise, he put one arm around my friend, the other arm around me, and pulled us close together toward him. Then this surprising Lord laughed in my heart's mind and I wanted to laugh as well, out loud. But the communion service was hardly the place for such holy frivolity!

This prayer can also be, then, the encouragement we need to work out the community of the family of God and become brothers and sisters, in purity.

We moderns live in an age of unnatural affections. Those chilling passages in Romans 1 describe our age perhaps better than any others in Scripture:

> Therefore God gave them over in the sinful desires of their hearts to sexual impurity for the degrading of their bodies with one another. They exchanged the truth of God for a lie, and worshiped and served created things rather than the Creator—who is forever praised (1:24-25).

Christ between you and me is the measurement for whether our loves are growing out of bounds in a trying age of overstimulated sexual affections. Few of us have an understanding of what powerful tools of prayer are available to us when we measure all human relationships in the presence of Christ, through the presence of Christ, and by the presence of Christ.

For instance, a young woman approached me. "Can I talk with you?" she asked, her voice hardly above a whisper. We went to the counseling room together, closed the door, and sat down.

Counseling rooms have become familiar places to me these last years. The itinerant minister becomes aware that people give to the ones who come and go the burdens that can't be given to the ones who stay. Because of the distance travel puts between me and them, I can be trusted to be a pain-bearer.

The young woman's story tumbled out, painfully, with stops and starts. I waited for her to come to the crux of her dilemma. I listened for the Holy Spirit whispering to my heart. She began to cry. Her tears flowed. We found a box of Kleenex. She wiped her eyes, blew her nose, and wept all the more.

Her story, when it was finally out, was a simple one. She was a young wife with a husband struggling through graduate school. Because they needed funds, she was working in a professional position. She had become sexually involved with a married man at her work. "I couldn't help myself. There was a pull stronger than what I can possibly describe." And then the weeping. "If my husband knew, it would destroy him. I love my husband—why has this happened to me?"

I have heard this story so often, with minor variations, that my tormented young woman has become an Everywoman, a type of those who have succumbed to the spirit of our age.

Has there ever been an age that worshiped the creature rather than the Creator more than ours? Other cultures worshiped idols, handmade gods who represented the supernatural world man could not understand. But our world is a man-centered world. We have abandoned the old idols. We no longer bow to works of stone or wood. We worship ourselves. We have transplanted the Creator with the created. When this happens, when the focus of our souls becomes fixated on ourselves rather than centering the thoughts, passions, and desires outward and upward toward the worship of God, we become perverted in our adoration, incestuous in our love of self.

"God gave them over to a depraved mind, to do what ought not to be done. . . . They have become filled with every kind of wickedness, evil, greed and depravity. . . . [They] exchanged natural relations for unnatural ones" (Romans 1:28, 29, 26). Do you see why I call this a chilling passage? It so aptly describes our own world though it was written centuries ago about the decadent culture of the Romans.

"Oh, that could never happen to me," says the bride, "I love my husband." So did the young woman weeping in the counseling room.

Consider carefully what I am saying: We live in a culture that is pervaded with a demonic persuasion of lust because the culture has given itself over to unnatural affections. No, even more. This culture of ours has called this spirit out, sought it, hunted after it, found it. Like the Romans, this twentieth-century culture, under the false name of sexual freedom, has become a catalog of unimaginable sexual evil.

In order to stand against it, we must be prepared. Ignorance will protect us no longer. We must develop the inner discipline of measuring all relationships in light of the protective presence of the living Christ.

Another wife brought her pain to me. The husband had submitted to the sexual advances of a woman at his work. Ashamed and humiliated and bewildered, he had brought this terrible information to her. Looking back, the two of them became aware that because of his Christian innocence, he was not prepared to deal with a world where people deliberately seduce one another. Through her tears, the young wife said, "This incident meant nothing to that woman. Going to bed with other men was standard activity to her. She had no idea that it was morally wrong."

Christ has given us a remarkable tool to combat the spirit of unnatural affection that pervades our age: the tool of mental fidelity. The state of our mind, not the state of our heart, is the primary key to faithfulness. This is the battlefield where we must gird ourselves in order to stand against the influence of an age which is keynoted by sexual lust. Christ taught,

> You have heard that it was said, "Do not commit adultery." But I tell you that anyone who looks at a woman lustfully has already committed adultery with her in his heart. If your right eye causes you to sin, gouge it out and throw it away. It is better for you to lose one part of your body than for your whole body to be thrown into hell (Matthew 5:27-29).

In other words, if you are thinking about someone in a sexual way, if your thoughts are toying with a forbidden desire, you are in danger of being overcome by the spirit of unnatural affections. You need to ask yourself: What would Christ say about this relationship? How would he feel about the words we use with each other? What would be his response if I ask him what to do? What happens when I place Christ between myself and this other to whom I'm attracted?

The mind is the key to our behavior. Desperate times require desperate actions. Pluck out of your life everything that is stimulating illegal desire. You can't rent a video cassette to catch a film at home you wouldn't want to go into a theater to see without tipping your hat to the demon of this age. You can't spend hours in front of the television allowing yourself to be titillated by bedroom scene after bedroom scene without being influenced by our culture. You cannot glance at pornographic magazines or books without stimulating unnatural desire.

Pluck it out, Christ instructs.

Our minds must be pure if we expect our bodies to remain pure as well. Search the Bible for as many verses as you can find which reveal God's attitude toward sexual purity. Then as a means of disciplining the mind, write down these passages in a notebook, word for word, and read them all when tempted.

Prayer is another effective tool. One year while attending a conference investigating "the religious component and healing" sponsored by members of the faculty of Duke University in Durham, North Carolina, I heard one psychiatrist emphasize that there is a bonding which occurs in the sexual relationship which is more than physical. It is a deep bonding which takes place on the emotional and psychic level. "Two bodies shall become one flesh," is a Scripture that describes something more significant than mere physical joining.

In cases of infidelity, either mental or physical, the psychiatrist explained, there is a bonding that occurs which disrupts God's normal intention for human relationships. A Christian himself, he mentioned that he used the prayer of severing to help these people who had become unnaturally bonded. The prayer of severing was helpful to the young wife, representing Everywoman, who shared her story with me in the counseling room.

This is a prayer that employs the powerful imagination. Many Christians are afraid of this tool and yet it is one of God's gifts to his children. There are ways the imagination may be misused; but when it is centered in Scripture and when its focus is Christ, it can free those who find themselves in sexual bondage.

Perhaps you are like my young friend weeping in the counseling room. You have become overwhelmed by a passion you seem helpless to control. Very simply, it is the evil influence of the lustful spirit of our age and you were not prepared to meet it. Now it has overcome you. It is the spirit of unnatural affection.

May I now, at this moment, introduce you to the One who is stronger than this bondage. Close your eyes in prayer. In your mind I want you to see Christ, your Lord. He is the One who is able to loose all bonds that tie us.

First, however, you need to confess your sin. You need to say to him, "Lord, I have sinned. Sinned against you and against my fellow man. I have committed adultery, either in my mind or in my body. I repent. I am sorry. I confess my sin, forgive me."

Now, in your mind, see three people. See yourself and the one to whom you are unnaturally bound. See the cords of bondage that bind you together. Now see Christ, the Christ of Revelation, "His head and hair were white like wool, as white as snow . . . his eyes were like blazing fire. . . . Out of his mouth came a sharp double-edged sword" (Revelation 1:14-16).

Hebrews 4:12-13 says,

> For the word of God is living and active. Sharper than any double-edged sword, it penetrates even to dividing soul and spirit, joints and marrow; it judges the thoughts and attitudes of the heart. Nothing in all creation is hidden from God's sight. Everything is uncovered and laid bare before the eyes of him to whom we must give account.

So you stand before this glistening One, Christ; and you are bound illicitly to another by your unnatural affections. And then Christ speaks the Word. It issues from his mouth, a shout, "Whatsoever you have loosed on earth will be loosed in heaven!" and that two-edged sword severs the cord, cuts the bindings, hacks apart the ties.

In your mind, you see that one to whom you were bound turn from you; and you, yourself, face Christ. You look into the brilliance of his gaze, he opens his arms and receives you unto himself. Scripture again tells us in Romans 8,

> Therefore, there is now no condemnation for those who are in Christ Jesus, because through Christ Jesus the law of the Spirit of life set me free from the law of sin and death. The mind of sinful man is death, but the mind controlled by the Spirit is life and peace (8:1-2, 6).

You may have to go through this cycle again and again; you may have to ask a trusted spiritual counselor to pray this prayer with you. But release will eventually come. You will be free indeed.

Christ between me and each person is the inner standard by which I am learning to judge all my human relationships.

The Christ Betwixt Thee and Me Prayer

Lord,
Be between child and me today,
Between myself and friend.
Hold my hand and the hand of the other also, Christ.
Walk in the middle as we walk.
Be the Word between us as we speak.
Lord, you be at the center of my loves.
Let all others be the radiating circumference.
Christ betwixt thee and me,
Betwixt me and thee, today I pray.
Amen.

The Discipline of Measuring Our Loves

Suggested passages for study and meditation: Matthew 12:33-37; Luke 6:43-45; 1 Thessalonians 4:3-8; 1 Peter 1:13-15, 4:1-4; Galatians 5:16-26; Proverbs 5, 6:20-35, 7, 9:13-18.

Hymns for meditation: "Where the Spirit of the Lord Is"
"When I Survey the Wondrous Cross"
"There's a Quiet Understanding"
"O the Deep, Deep Love of Jesus"

I believe God wants to teach me more about measuring my loves because:

This concept is not new; I have previously learned something about measuring my loves when:

The Scripture(s) God is impressing upon my heart that underscores this discipline is written out below.

What this Scripture means in terms of my personal situation is:

Other incidents have come to bear on my learning process: I have read something in a book; a friend spoke a pertinent word; my memory was jogged about an almost forgotten event. Such additional experiences are:

As an indication of my intent to develop this inner discipline, I will pray "The Christ between Thee and Me Prayer." I have prayed the prayer

(circle the appropriate numbers):

Seven days, twice a day

1 2 3 4 5 6 7 8 9 10 11 12 13 14

Thirty days, once a day

1 2 3 4 5 6 7 8 9 10 11 12 13 14

15 16 17 18 19 20 21 22 23 24 25 26 27 28 29 30

During the above learning time frame, the friend I will share this learning process with is:

7

SACRIFICING OUR ISAACS:

The Discipline of Giving Back What We Love

A woman who lost her twenty-year-old daughter to cancer responded to my words of sympathy by saying, "It was hard. But I attempted to offer my child back to God in the same way she was given to me—with love." I was amazed by her response, and moved. Many times since, I have prayed that if I were ever required to do the same, I would also be able to say, "Here, Lord. I give to you this precious one in the same way he was given to me—with love, with love."

I do understand that this kind of faithful response can only come through a lifetime of obedient practice.

I remember when Melissa, our daughter, suffered from a fever of unidentified origin while she was in junior high. A mother of four children, I was pretty well accustomed to colds and stomach aches and influenzas; but I discovered that one's belief in God is tested at these times when children are seriously ill. Melissa's fever regularly fluctuated between 100 and 102 degrees; there were no accompanying symptoms apart from fatique, and though she was tested and hospitalized, and tested and re-tested, and threatened with hospitalization again, not even the best of doctors could locate the cause of her infection. A nagging conversational memory reminded me that a medical friend had once said that 50 percent of FUO's—fever of unknown origin—ended in death.

In the middle of this long two months when the tests came back negative regarding mononucleosis and the other normal run-of-the-mill things, I realized we weren't dealing with a five-day virus—we might be facing something terminal. I woke one night in a cold sweat, went downstairs, took my Bible and my notebook and began to do battle within my soul. Could I offer my child, this precious and only daughter, to the perfect, workable will of God? Could I allow him to do in her life and in ours whatever he saw fit, and to make each of us into the people he desired?

My prayer notebook records the end of that long night of struggle: "Lord, someone I love is ill. I have a terror, Father, a terror of some latent debilitating disease and yet I trust in your inimitable, perfect goodness. I know there is nothing that comes into our life but what you allow it. I have given you my children. I bring to you again this child, my daughter Melissa. She is your child, simply on loan to us. I praise you for whatever you are working in her life and in ours."

Like Abraham, I had offered up my child. From that point on, for the next month and a half as more and more possibilities loomed, I was unafraid.

Unlike the story of many parents, our child was restored to normal health. But that moment was a Moriah experience for me; a beginning understanding that the Isaac prayer of sacrifice is one which must be prayed, again and again, in different areas of my life.

There is perhaps no more moving scriptural account than the one from Genesis 22, where Abraham hears the voice of God calling to him, "Abraham! Take your son, your only son, Isaac, whom you love, and go to the region of Moriah. Sacrifice him there as a burnt offering on one of the mountains I will tell you about." What a momentous message for any parent to hear! Abraham had waited a lifetime for this child. Isaac was the fulfillment of God's earlier promise to Abraham that he, through this heir, would be the father, the progenitor, of a great nation.

Scripture is filled with passages of drama, but none more portentous than this, "Early the next morning Abraham got up and saddled his donkey. He took with him two of his servants and his son Isaac. When he had cut enough wood for the burnt offering, he set out for the place God had told him about."

Imagine yourself hearing that dark word come from the Lord about someone you hold dear, some child who brings delight to your life, some grandchild. Imagine how terrible the thought of the knife. Imagine how many times you consider which will be the least painful way to slay your beloved. Think of the culture that surrounds you. Think of the frequent and horrible practice of human sacrifice. Taste the blackness that seeps into your soul because you thought you served a God different than the pagan deities with their insatiable bloodlust. Plod on, old one, shriveled and gaunt with age. Plod on. Can you offer Isaac up in the same way he was given to you?

I can't read this passage without marveling at Abraham's obedience. Commentators often remark about his faith—he responds to Isaac's question about the absent lamb by saying, "God himself will provide the lamb for the burnt offering, my son." But I wonder if at that moment Abraham's faith wasn't numb. Mine would have been. Wasn't his old heart beating wildly? His intellect groping for past remembrances of the God he had known? I suspect, at least at certain moments in this journey into sacrifice, that it was sheer blind obedience that propelled the father.

And I understand why God waited for old age to test the faithfulness of Abraham's love. It takes a lifetime of practice to offer up to God what we cherish most.

At different journeying posts in each of our lives, God asks us to give up to him the current object we love. He tests our willingness; he tests our obedience. Scripture says, "Some time later God tested Abraham. He said to him, 'Abraham! Take your son, your only son, Isaac, whom you love.'"

It's important for parents to walk to this spiritual altar, to offer their children back to the Lord. For many of us, this begins when they are infants. We give them to God in a dedicatory service or through a christening ceremony. We give them up to the Lord, sometimes on that first day of school watching them walk away from home, looking so small, so vulnerable before the enormous destructive forces that range the world. We suddenly realize we are not all-powerful but are dependent upon supernatural intervention to protect our child from oncoming cars, from the cruelty on the playground, from harsh teachers. At each point of a child's growth, they leave us by degrees, and we must learn to give them again into God's hands.

But it's not just children we must learn to offer up. All the objects we hold dear require *intentional* sacrifice; and willing repetition seems a requirement in this walk toward obedience. I remember the night when, after years of struggle, after years of discipline and self-denial, I had received the first copies of my first book. I heard that divine voice whispering to me, "Can you give to me your Isaac? Can you give to me your writing?"

In shock, I responded (like Abraham, lifting my eyes to that place afar off), "Lord, you wouldn't ask me not to write, would you?"

The question came, adamant again without equivocation or pandering explanations: "Can you give to me your Isaac?" (God never converses when he has something explicit, something direct to ask of us.)

I sighed. Of course I would offer up this thing I loved. I prepared the ass and stacked the wood and went plodding with a heavy heart to that far mountain. Fortunately, my writing was not required of me, just the existential intent of sacrifice; an important distinction to God. I have written and written since that dark encounter with the Lord.

I have had to sacrifice so many Isaacs of so many kinds. My heart is a clutching heart, an owning heart, a proprietor's heart. I have had to offer up my love for my husband, my pride in a new home, my sense of satisfaction in the ability to earn my financial keep in the family, my fixation with a current creative project. There are people I love too much, positions that threaten my single-eyed devotion, cherished affections that dim the memory of that ancient proclamation: "Hear, O Israel: the LORD our God, the LORD is one. Love the LORD your God with all your heart and with all your soul and with all your strength. Do not follow other gods, the gods of the peoples around you" (Deuteronomy 6:4-5, 14).

Why is this sacrificial prayer so important?

Because we humans are always in danger: the people we love, the possessions we love, the professions we love threaten to supplant the place in our soul God reserves for himself. He desires our whole heart. But at our very essence we are idolatrous. We need to learn to offer up the Isaacs of our lives in the same way the gifts were given to us—with love, with love. Imagine God's delight when he watched Abraham actually place the kindling and wood on the pile of stones, when the old man sharpened his knife and turned toward his son. Finally! At last! Here was one man intent on following God.

Abraham's unnatural intent is eventually thwarted by the divine provision of a substitute ram, thicket-trapped, for the sacrifice. Reading the account, one can almost hear God sing "I will surely bless you and make your descendants as numerous as the stars in the sky and as the sand on the seashore . . . and through your offspring all nations on earth will be blessed, because you have obeyed me."

God always requires the intentional sacrifice of anything cherished, of any of the children of my creative womb—the work of my hands, the labor of my heart, the sweat of my soul. I am learning to sacrifice them before he asks, to gather the wood, to go to the mountain.

Every summer the Christian Booksellers Association holds a huge trade show which presents new products—books, records, curricula, jewelry, videos—from the religious publishing concerns to buyers. The convention is held either in Anaheim, Dallas, or Washington, D.C. since these are three of the few United States cities with a convention hall large enough to house the eight thousand attendees, a group that rivals the size of its comparable secular organization, the American Booksellers Association.

I find that I am often out of sorts at these conventions and I attempt to avoid them as much as possible. The temptations are all too real to me—the vaulting ego, the need for peer approval, the desire to be known and recognized. At the last CBA I attended, I saw a young man wearing a commentary on his lapel; he had fashioned a self-made button which read, "I Am a VERY Famous Author." I thought his humorous, satirical approach summarized what so many of us were inwardly tempted to feel. Autograph parties. Celebrity treatment. Prizes. My temperament does not weather this hoopla very well, and though I am sure many people remember that the Christian book industry is ministry first and foremost, that reality tends to fade for me. I generally crawl home investigating the bruises on my soul from being known or from being unknown.

Two books were the result of last year's labor, and I recognized a need to offer them up in some formalized way. Though I had prayed over them privately, I wanted some outward action to accompany my inward sacrifice. Discussing this desire with my pastor, he found a means for me out of our church's liturgical formalities called "The Long Dedication." A date was arranged when during morning prayers I could present these creative children to God.

Strangely blissful, I checked the family schedule. All four children, one husband, and my daughter's boyfriend were free to accompany me on my glad journey to the land of Moriah. I planned a picnic breakfast for this morning's journey—I packed (into a basket) hard-boiled eggs, melon slices, bagels and cream cheese, homemade coffee cake; poured juice into a cooler and coffee into a thermos and set out with a singing heart and the people I love. We parked by the river, spread the cloth, and ate with laughter; what a joyful sacrifice this was becoming.

In the church that morning were my family, the pastor, his wife and child (who rang the hand-pulled bell), the church secretary, and the lay-reader and his wife.

After morning prayers which fittingly, for me, honored the life of Thomas à Kempis, I laid my two books on the altar in the nave as family and friends held in their hands passouts headed "An Offering to the Lord of Two Books by Karen Burton Mains." I read aloud the introductory words on the paper: "I present to you these books to be set apart for the Glory of God." I thought, *Everyone I know in the Christian book industry is at the Christian Booksellers Convention, and here am I in this little place, happy among these few people, with a child ringing the clarion announcement which only this neighborhood can hear. I would not trade places for all the prizes or recognition in the world.*

For the first time, I understood God's blessings on us when we offer up our Isaacs. The blessings of God upon us when we intentionally yield up our loves is this: He receives our offering. He takes it from our hand. He welcomes our work. He embraces our loves. He makes these dear, these precious things, his own.

And in that moment, unlike any other, we know that we are blessed; and at that point I began to understand *what does not happen* when we don't offer up the sacrifice of those things we cherish most; we don't experience the intense, bounding joy of knowing that God has received our loves into his hand.

Do you have an Isaac you should offer today? Is there something too dear, too precious, that holds a grip on your heart? You'll never know a blessing compared to the one that takes place when God receives your sacrifice. Prepare the wood. Saddle the ass. Turn your eyes to that far-off land. Begin the lifelong pilgrimage. Offer up what you love in the same way it was given to you—with love.

The Sacrificing Your Isaac Prayer

Lord,
Here is the work of my mind, my heart, my hand.
Here is the fruit of my womb,
Here is the love of my life.

I lay them on the altar of sacrifice.
I withdraw my hand.
I turn my eyes to your face, my One true God.

I give this cherished thing up to you
the way it was given to me,
with love, with love.
And gladly.
Amen.

THE DISCIPLINE OF GIVING BACK WHAT WE LOVE

Suggested passages for study and meditation: Genesis 22:1-18; Exodus 20:3; Hebrews 12:1-2; Matthew 13:44-45; Luke 14:25-35; Matthew 10:37-39

Hymns for meditation: "Only One Life to Offer"
"Whiter than Snow"
"Living for Jesus"
"Something for Thee"

I believe God wants to teach me more about giving back to Him what I love because:

This concept is not new; I have previously learned something about relinquishment when:

The Scripture(s) God is impressing upon my heart that underscores this discipline is written out below.

What this Scripture means in terms of my personal situation is:

Other incidents have come to bear on my learning process: I have read something in a book; a friend spoke a pertinent word; my memory was jogged about an almost forgotten event. Such additional experiences are:

As an indication of my intent to develop this inner discipline, I will pray "The Sacrificing Your Isaac Prayer." I have prayed the prayer

(circle the appropriate numbers):

Seven days, twice a day

1 2 3 4 5 6 7 8 9 10 11 12 13 14

Thirty days, once a day

1 2 3 4 5 6 7 8 9 10 11 12 13 14

15 16 17 18 19 20 21 22 23 24 25 26 27 28 29 30

During the above learning time frame, the friend I will share this learning process with is:

8

ON BEING EDITED:

The Discipline of Welcoming Corrections

Having experienced childbearing, I am often amazed at how similar writing a book is to having a baby. An idea is planted in the author's mind and a creative conception has occurred. This grows from a tiny seed to a huge weight which must be nurtured prenatally until it is birthed from the imaginative womb, pages and pages of words, with a personality totally its own—one that often amazes the writer who has conceived it.

But just as with a new baby, the work really begins when the infant is brought home to the publishing house. Here editors analyze its condition. Reading consultants lend their opinions; marketing people project the newborn's future prospects. Graphic artists doctor it. Printers and designers are called in to advise.

And as much work as all this is, I personally feel positive about the process, because I believe the Christian publishing industry—writers, editors, publishers, publicists—should all function together as the body of Christ, with uniquely gifted people contributing their specialties and abilities to the raising of the little child.

Admittedly, editing can be a terrifying process. This is the infant I have nurtured and loved and carried close to my heart for many months. This is the child I went to bed thinking about and woke up the next morning thinking about. I have often lived the life of my creative child. Now someone is tampering with my twentieth draft. Someone is editing my baby. All that blue pencil! All those editorial notes in the columns. The first chapter has been reinserted midpoint; the last has become the first. Will I or my child ever survive?

Maxwell Perkins is considered by some to have been the consummate editor. Surely no one in American literature has remained so important yet so unknown. Associated for over thirty-six years with one publishing firm, Charles Scribner's Sons, he changed the known approach to editing. Not only did he involve himself in the works of his authors, he involved himself in their lives as well. He became banker, confidant, counselor, father figure, and friend. He either discovered or helped to develop the writing of greats such as Hemmingway, Fitzgerald, Thomas Wolfe, Ring Lardner, Marjorie Kinning Rawlings, Erskine Caldwell, Taylor Caldwell, Alan Paton, and James Jones.

He not only discovered and published authors, he changed the literary culture of his time. Few editors before him had done so much work on submitted manuscripts, but he attempted to remain faithful to his credo: The book belongs to the author. "An author's work comes entirely from himself. An editor does not add to a book. At best he serves as a handmaiden to an author. Don't ever get to feeling important about yourself because at best an editor at most releases energy. He creates nothing. The process is so simple. If you have a Mark Twain, don't try and make him into a Shakespeare or make a Shakespeare into a Mark Twain."[1]

I insist on this editorial process; I've even written this process into some of my contracts. I want to work with my editor to produce the healthiest baby possible. I want to be present, indeed active, during the operation.

I hand my editor my cherished, cried-over, prayed-over manuscript. She reads it. She invites other advisors to read it. They make suggestions. Then she edits the pages. She uses her pencil. She uses her scissors. She clips, scotch tapes, and rearranges passages. Then I receive a phone call. I bring my copy of the manuscript. Page by page, edit by edit, line by line, we go over the two manuscripts. I insist on restoring; my editor yields. She insists on keeping changes; I yield.

"What do you mean by this word?" she demands. I am forced to defend the meaning or change the word. "I don't understand this character," she challenges me. I rewrite. We cut and tape; we bang out a new passage on the computer.

"But you have changed the meaning of the symbol here!" I protest. She relents but forces me to make myself more clear. We compromise. She erases and writes in our corrections. We think of better ways to say what is being said. She erases again. We sharpen our pencils. We blow mounds of eraser dust off the desk. We check each story against each full-color illustration. We make notes to the artist. Lunch break. We shove aside papers and eat at the desk. My brain is beginning to suffer fatigue. There are six more chapters to go.

The whole afternoon continues in the same way, and finally we are finished. We always pronounce any work we do together as a "classic." And for me the normal pattern is to go home, be blue for several days, wonder why I ever thought I could write, and vow never to write again.

On Being Edited

Now that I am more confident in my own writing abilities, I lean less and less on my editorial relationships and more on my own developing craft and skills. I am less editorially dependent; and paradoxically, more editorially respectful. Experienced writers are usually assigned to the head of the editorial department, someone who has undergone this arduous process with hundreds of manuscripts. I trust his or her eye and training to see deficiencies in my child that I have overlooked despite my watchfulness.

But the editorial stage is only an early part of the process. Once the edited manuscript has been typed, the next stage of development is putting the manuscript on a computer disk that finally matures into galleys, then proofs, where the type has been set and photographed and where any last minute changes are extremely expensive to make. The growth process for raising the child I have birthed to publishing maturity has taken months.

Why have I submitted myself to this lengthy torture? Because I want to be part of creating the best book possible. If my editor doesn't understand my child, neither will my readers. I am dealing with truth; I want the meaning to be clear. I submit to this process because I love my child. I want this infant to make as significant a contribution in the world as he is able to make. A good editor, a good publishing concern, makes that possible. And while working together—a good editor alongside a good author—perhaps a minor or major work of art will be created to the glory of God.

You and I are going through another editing process: our lives are being edited.

This concept was beautifully expressed at my mother's funeral. Mother was a published poet of two books of poetry. She had served for many years as the editor of a national literary magazine. At the time of her death she was president of the Chicago branch of Poets and Patrons. The family friend who conducted her funeral service and preached the sermon had been my writing professor in college. He said: "Each Christian is a poem of God. This insight from the Holy Spirit was expressed by the apostle Paul in these words to the Ephesians in chapter 2:10 'We are his workmanship.' We have taken the Greek word for workmanship into our English language bodily, without even translating it. The word is *poema*; we say poem. 'For we are his workmanship, created in Christ Jesus for good works, which God prepared beforehand, that we should walk in them.' What is a poem? 'A composition characterized by great beauty of language or thought,' says the dictionary."

Listening carefully, I thought how appropriate this funeral sermon was for my mother. Dr. Lorentzen closed with these words, "God has just completed his poem entitled 'Wilma Burton' and his purpose is fulfilled in her. She has undergone the last revision. For her, all patterns are perfect now. Rhythm, rhyme, and metaphor fit together beautifully and make marvelous sense. She has been entered in the Lord's own anthology of finished works. We came in today thinking of Wilma, God's poem. Let us go out thinking of God, who wants to make each of us a work of art."

I, Karen Burton Mains, am being edited by my Heavenly Editor for needless repetitions, for wasted meaning. He takes his blue pencil to the very marrow of my soul and crosses out anything unworthy of the *poema* he is creating out of me. His eraser is at work, too—death and loss and grief. Self-pity and jealousy and deception are all being removed and rewritten in such a way that the end product will have its fullest intended content. Sections that don't really belong to my story and don't comply with my Editor's idea of a finished work are being deleted. I cry out, "Oh, that hurts!" I protest, "But I loved that little sin, that private attitude."

My Editor knows what he is doing. He is making a work of art out of raw stuff, the unpredictable human entity that is Karen Burton Mains. And like any editor of genius, this Divine One is not attempting to make me into anyone else but myself.

What is my role in this? I must cooperate with the Divine Editor. I must put away my defense mechanisms, my rationalizations, my denials. I must admit my faults. I must stop lying to myself and to others, insisting that I am what I am not, or am not what I really am. I must become vulnerable, seek corrections, find the nub of truth in each criticism and apply it. I must force myself to be continually on a growth edge, learning in new areas I haven't tried before. I must welcome the adjustments people attempt to make in my behavior as well as the godly modifications that come through the suggestions of Scripture. I must learn from my children, my spouse, my friends, my employer, my pastor. I must see myself as a student in life.

I recently ran into one of these mid-course corrections.

I often care for people in pain and want to make myself available to bear their sorrows in whatever ways I can.

"Is he leaning too hard on you?" asked my husband about a friend.

"Oh, no!" I instantly replied and thought to myself, *But if he does, it is my fault because I would be allowing him to lean too hard on me.*

Several months later I hit one of those fatigue barrens we all wander through when we have overdone, and it seemed suddenly as though *everyone* was leaning on me. I asked a friend to do a favor while I was traveling. When I returned home and this task had been forgotten I became (privately) furious—an anger I recognized to be disproportionate to the incident and complicated by my own weariness.

While discussing this response with another friend and asking for counsel in the situation, I remembered my own previous thoughts, *If he leans too hard on me, it is my fault.*

"You know," said my friend, "you give people the impression that you have hours to listen to them."

I considered that to be a compliment, but realized the truth might be that I gave people the impression that I had hours to listen to them and didn't need mutuality, a give-and-take, a serve-one-another-sharing.

I went home determined to adjust the balance in my relationships. The very man who had forgotten to do one small thing for me called, and I casually slipped into the conversation a comment about the tightness of my schedule. He responded instantly, volunteered to help me, and lifted a load from my shoulders. Just like that!

The truth is: I focus on other people's pain, and neglect to pay attention to my own. This can have disastrous results in terms of the exhaustion I experience, not to mention the imbalance in relationships.

Cooperating with my Divine Editor means that I work together with him in the editing process.

So must you dear friend, so must you. Each Christian must learn to submit to and cooperate with God's editing process if his life is to be made into a *poema*, a "composition characterized by great beauty." Oh, you can be content with a hack job, a do-it-yourself published edition, or pencil scratches on the back of an envelope discarded unread after your death, but I think every human longs to live a life of significance, at least in some small way.

God makes of each of his creations a significant statement. We must learn to welcome God's editing process in our lives; we must not only welcome his work but also submit and cooperate with it if we are to become something more than a pulp novel . . . tossed aside, forgotten because of its inferior style.

1. A. Scott Berg, *Max Perkins: Editor of Genius* (New York: Dutton, 1978), p. 6.

The Prayer for Being Edited

Lord,
Edit me.
Correct me when my words are faulty.
Revise my thoughts.
Polish the rough passages of my being.

Submit me to a review panel who can judge
my strengths and weaknesses.
Correct the internal rhythm
so that the outward meter will be whole.
I want to be a work of art, Lord, a classic of some kind.

Give me form.
Fill me with the beauty of yourself.
Help those who read my life to see
that you are the workman;
I am the workmanship;
and out of me you are creating a work of art.
Amen.

The Discipline of Welcoming Corrections

Suggested passages for study and meditation: Proverbs 3:11-12; Psalm 94:12, 119:75; Hebrews 12:5-6, 9-11; John 15:1-17; Matthew 3:8, 10.

Hymns for meditation: "O to Be Like Thee!"
"Breathe on Me, Breath of God"
"Have Thine Own Way,Lord"
"Spirit of God Descend upon My Heart"

I believe God wants to teach me more about welcoming corrections because:

This concept is not new; I have previously learned something about the Lord's discipline when:

The Scripture(s) God is impressing upon my heart that underscores this discipline is written out below.

What this Scripture means in terms of my personal situation is:

Other incidents have come to bear on my learning process: I have read something in a book; a friend spoke a pertinent word; my memory was jogged about an almost forgotten event. Such additional experiences are:

As an indication of my intent to develop this inner discipline, I will pray "The Prayer for Being Edited." I have prayed the prayer

(circle the appropriate numbers):

Seven days, twice a day

1 2 3 4 5 6 7 8 9 10 11 12 13 14

Thirty days, once a day

1 2 3 4 5 6 7 8 9 10 11 12 13 14

15 16 17 18 19 20 21 22 23 24 25 26 27 28 29 30

During the above learning time frame, the friend I will share this learning process with is:

9

THE GOD HUNT:

The Discipline of Finding God in the Everyday

One Fall I took a fungi identification course. Every autumn my family and I had watched the fringed bracket fungus spread its orange and yellow layers over a decaying oak stump. A friend, knowledgeable in the ways of field and forest, had introduced us to the culinary delights of the puffball, and admittedly, my motivation for attending this class stemmed from the desire to learn which mushrooms growing in the woods surrounding my home were edible and which were killers. So I found myself one evening with other fungi identifiers (all seemingly normal folk like myself) in a gleaming laboratory in a scientific center at the nearby arboretum.

The very first words our professor said were, "The purpose of this course is not to identify which mushrooms are edible. The purpose is to learn to identify fungi to the classification of genus." Well, so much for my plans about homegrown gourmet menus; but with twenty-two dollars already committed, I decided to submit myself to the scientific approach.

The professor required that we bring fungi samples to class each week—so I went into the woods with the recommended mushroom-hunting equipment in hand: a stiff basket large enough to hold the biggest specimens without piling them on top of each other; a digging tool—a small trowel or a sturdy penknife; a notebook for writing down details of collection sites; small tie-on labels, plastic bags, and a hand lens. I had been instructed to bring back a good portion of the root system in order to classify properly, and also to procure plain white paper for making spore prints. (We were told to include a whistle to be used in case of emergencies; but since our nearby woods are only one hundred feet square, there wasn't much danger in becoming lost, so I eliminated this safety feature.)

I learned that the best mushroom field guides are the ones that don't have pictures. Photographs are often misleading because of the lighting conditions or the variable coloring due to the age of the fungi. One properly identifies a mushroom by the way the universal veil (the membrane which covers the cap and stem in the mushroom's button state) tears and by what kind of fleshy remnants are left on the mature sporocarp (the top). One also makes classification by determining whether the fungi has pores or gills and then by making a spore print.

Spore prints fascinate me. The identifier slices the stem from the mushroom cap and places the cap with the gill or spore side (depending on the nature of the fungi) down flat on a plain white piece of paper. In a little while the spores drop, leaving a print beneath the cap which, when it is lifted, reveals a dotted sprinkling of different colors—black or cream or pink or brownish red. This print is the primary key to placing the speciman in the proper genus. By the time I'd made my first spore print, I didn't care whether or not my mushrooms were edible. I'd suddenly been introduced to a new and fascinating sub-species of nature. When the fungi next sprouted in my woods, I was like a child wild to race out on a treasure hunt.

Nature always presents us with interesting illustrations to participating in the spiritual world. One Scripture passage, 1 John 4:13-16, has often baffled me with its mystical implications,

> We know that we live in him and he in us, because he has given us of his Spirit. And we have seen and testify that the Father has sent his Son to be the Savior of the world. If any one acknowledges that Jesus is the Son of God, God lives in him and he in God. And so we know and rely on the love God has for us. God is love. Whoever lives in love lives in God, and God in him.

I am of the very human inclination that wants to know how this happens—*Oh yeah, give me a for instance,* I think. *Show me. Give me a tangible example.* My mycological examinations did just that; they gave me a mold-smelling, earthy, spore-bearing paradigm.

Mushrooms have a habit of appearing suddenly as if from nowhere. But what we term a mushroom is actually only the fruiting body of a vast network of fungal life which is mostly under the ground but present in the soil year round. These fruiting bodies—identified as the common puffball, the fly agaric, the ink cap—are comparable to flowers that grow on a bush, except in the case of the fungi, all the vegetative growth is subterranean.

Fungal cells take the form of long filaments known as hypae which duplicate and grow and eventually become a dense mat which produces the energy for the formation of the fruiting state. A microscopic bud forms on this organic fabric, then another. The buds grow to become fleshy buttons which push up through the soil and grow into fairy rings, or field mushrooms, or stinkhorns.

And lo and behold! Here comes a mushroom hunter with a basket in hand. She spots a tempting clump of Caesar's Mushrooms and with her tool loosens them from the soil, root and all. She marvels at the dense mat of fibers which have produced these fruiting bodies. The hunter has a find, something new to be classified in the laboratory. (She has more of a find than she knows, because her professor is aware that this species of mushrooms is edible, and despite his earlier disclaimer he will wash them in the laboratory sink and cook them with butter in an electric frying pan and share tasty succulent slices with the class.)

The apostle John says, "Whoever lives in love lives in God, and God in him." That sounds very well and good, but how does a spiritual hunter make this specific? What does abiding mean? How does one go abiding? What exactly does this passive activity look like?

Abiding in God is a lot like the experience I had when I took my fungi identification course. I began to see fungi everywhere I looked. There were boletus at my front door, lichen on the quartered rounds in the wood pile, bracket fungi growing on almost every tree, strands of fungal mycelium on woodland logs. Because my amateur eye had been trained, I began to see the fungi life in the world, all around me.

The helpful book, *The Encyclopedia of Mushrooms*, reads "Not all fungi form mushrooms. Most are mold fungi which remain microscopic throughout their lives. Literally thousands of microscopic molds can be isolated from the soil, dung, plant and animal remains, and even from streams, rivers, and the edge of the sea. Their tiny spores are present everywhere in the dust and have been found high up in the atmosphere."

It seems as though fungi are everpresent, and as our primary Sunday school lessons taught us, so is God.

We need to learn how to discover the One about whom John writes, "We know that we live in him and he in us, because he has given us of his own Spirit." Years ago, David and I devised a spiritual game (read discipline) for ourselves and our children by which we could learn to identify God in all of life: the God Hunt. The purpose for this game was to motivate our family to make God sightings. Because of this identification we could sense we were abiding in God existentially and that he was abiding in us. Any time God intervenes in our everyday world and we recognize it to be him, we say, "I spy."

Practically, God can be identified (1) through answered prayer, (2) through unexpected evidence of his care, (3) through help to do his work in the world, and (4) through any unusual linkage or timing. David and I record these evidences of divine activity in our prayer journals. With twenty some years of disciplined prayer records and a stack of spiral ring notebooks as evidence, it would be impossible to convince me that God is uninvolved in my life. There are many times when he seems silent, and certainly immovable, but I have learned that he is always there.

Lest I be guilty of dealing in generalities, let me illustrate these four areas of discovery out of the pages of my latest journal.

Answered prayer requests: Most of us don't know when God answers our prayers because we don't have a system of writing and recording our requests. In the prayer request section of my journal I keep numbered lists of items I bring before the Lord; then when a prayer is answered, I make a notation in the corresponding column giving the date or the means or the way God answered my prayer.

One dramatic answered request involved an unsuitable employee who wielded executive power in an organization that influenced the future of our broadcast ministry. One day we were notified through an intermediary that, along with several other Christian leaders whom we greatly admire, David's and my name had been deleted from the list of approved authors for the organization's monthly periodical. Realizing that you "can't please all the people all the time," I nevertheless felt that the style in which this was handled indicated an un-Christlike disposition to arrogance which was bound to have seeping ramifications in other areas.

I felt strongly led to pray for this man's removal. A year later he was released from his post, and we heard stories of other disturbing misappropriations of power. A letter of apology soon came requesting that we consider our relationship with this organization restored.

Through such dramatic evidences one discovers God's intervention in the everyday of life. Scripture actually asks us to pray for those who persecute us—but I believe this incident was allowed to happen so that I could be obedient to that inner voice of the Spirit to bind the power of the enemy as he worked disorder in a fine Christian organization through the machinations of one human.

Unexpected evidence of his care: As a former pastor's wife, I am well aware of the neglect that occurs in the lives of those called to full-time ministry. Either through our own fault in not allowing our weaknesses to show, or through the neglect from those to whom we minister, some of the neediest people in the land are the ordained and their spouses. David and I have devoted much of our spare time to loving and encouraging the men and women who are our ministering peers; but one is always a little surprised when submerged pain begins to surface in oneself. I have faced death and grief and adolescent-raising and the vagaries of public ministry with little (actually next-to-no) outside spiritual direction.

Having learned to go it alone, to be a woman of independent emotional and spiritual means, I was not prepared to *need* this pastoral ministry! But I did. My prayer notebook records two years of prayers of gratitude. I have been prayed for when sick and discouraged and fearful. Communion has been brought to me when I was desperately fatigued from public itinerant ministry. Words of encouragement have been spoken that cheered me. The staff of our local church has even read my books. David and I have been allowed to slowly find our place; no one has overwhelmed us with added responsibility. I have been anointed with oil for healing. I have been held accountable. We, ministers of the Gospel of Christ, have been ministered to by ministers of the Gospel of Christ. And that of course, is the way it always should be.

Help to do God's work in the world: Often, evidence of God in our everyday world is joint and ligament to another area in which we can identify God. Because I experienced divine care mediated through loving humans, I am free to receive love and give love to man and to God in a way I was not able to do three years ago. I have become strong and spiritually feisty, ready to take on more difficult journeys in this spiritual adventure of the walk of faith because of the inner healing brought by faithful men and women.

We also see God helping us do his work in the world in some of the most common activities. A morning of cooking yields two casseroles, one to serve this evening, one to freeze. Then word comes that a friend's family is undergoing stress of some sort. There is extra food to share, how wonderful. Acquaintances cancel plans, leaving us with two extra tickets for a sports event. A neighbor begins to talk of her troubled marriage; we can invite her and her husband to spend the evening with us (at a sports activity he happens to avidly follow). Hand-me-down clothes in good condition, plants from an over-productive herb garden, a special buy from a factory outlet store—the sharing of these material gifts often paves the way to bring glimpses of God to others. A quickly jotted note, an impulsive phone call, a spontaneous hug—suddenly we find the simple act has deep meaning. Through countless kindnesses, large and small, we become agents of God's care.

Unusual linkage or timing: These are the situations which are labeled "circumstances" but which for the Christian are evidences that God is Master Chess Player, taking years sometimes to bring his plans into a coordinated pattern. Recently, in discussion with publishers about the best way to market a book, David and I felt that the primary target audience was the local pastor who would be most benefited if church people put into practice the message of this particular product. Ideally, we decided, we would like to test the concepts in one urban center, coordinating our efforts with local pastors and with the broadcast outlets in that area. We named our ideal city. Three hours after we had ended this conference call, the president of a large seminary in the area we had named phoned David inviting him to speak at a pastor's conference and asked if the

Lord had laid anything special on his heart to say to those ministers. "How about testing this concept?" my husband inquired. His suggestion was met with enthusiasm.

How do we find God in our everyday lives? By deliberately seeking him. When we deliberately hunt for anything, for mushrooms or for God, we begin to find what we seek in every area of life. Going on the God Hunt means that we develop an awareness that these divine sightings are only the fruiting bodies of his Presence. The rest of the fact of God's omnipresence is like the fungi *mycelium*, a dense mat of fibers, strands of filaments which are a network in the unseen world. These divine sightings are only the flowers of a supernatural vegetative life, a web of godliness which networks in the spiritual world. As we hunt for them, we can find them; we can learn to recognize them for what they are.

Deliberately setting out to sight the fruiting bodies, even blowing the whistle to signal "That was God! I found him!" is a practical means by which we begin to "live in him and he in us."

The God Hunt Prayer

Lord,
Help me to hunt for you
and find you in my everyday world.
Give me a hunger for yourself
that cannot be satisfied by
any other thing.
Amen.

The Discipline of Finding God in the Everyday

Suggested passages for study and meditation: Jeremiah 29:13, Deuteronomy 4:29, Isaiah 55:6; Psalm 19:1-7, 139; Isaiah 64:3.

Hymns for meditation: "Be Thou My Vision"
"Immortal, Invisible God Only Wise"
"I Sing the Mighty Power of God"
"Open My Eyes"

I believe God wants to teach me more about identifying his presence in my life every day because:

This concept is not new; I have previously learned something about discovering God in the every day when:

The Scripture(s) God is impressing upon my heart that underscores this discipline is written out below.

What this Scripture means in terms of my personal situation is:

Other incidents have come to bear on my learning process: I have read something in a book; a friend spoke a pertinent word; my memory was jogged about an almost forgotten event. Such additional experiences are:

Because I believe God wants me to be more aware of his presence in my life, I determine to go on a God Hunt every day for 30 days. I will write my God sighting in a journal.

____yes ____no

As an indication of my intent to develop this inner discipline, I will pray "The God Hunt Prayer." I have prayed the prayer

(circle the appropriate numbers):

Seven days, twice a day

1 2 3 4 5 6 7 8 9 10 11 12 13 14

Thirty days, once a day

1 2 3 4 5 6 7 8 9 10 11 12 13 14

15 16 17 18 19 20 21 22 23 24 25 26 27 28 29 30

During the above learning time frame, the friend I will share this learning process with is:

10

PRISON ON OUR BACKS:

The Discipline of Choosing Freedom from the Need for Human Approval

For years I have had a love/hate relationship with what has come to be known as the Christian speaker's circuit—that round of Christian retreats and Bible conferences to which I frequently receive invitations to speak. I love the ministry opportunities, but I hate the subtle temptations to sin which any public position affords to my frail and most human of egos.

It sounds glamorous, doesn't it?—all that attention, people coming to a large hall to hear you speak, traveling, flying from

Chicago to Boston, to Miami, to Los Angeles. It sounds glamorous, but, at least for me, the very fact that it sounds glamorous is terrifying.

The negative potential of notoriety became apparent to me early when I was a main speaker for one of my first large meetings, a gathering of four thousand women on a state university campus. It was one of the first times I heard my name whispered as I passed through the crowded foyer to make my way backstage—*That's Karen Mains. She's our speaker.* It was one of the first times people actually stood in line for me to autograph their books. It was the very first time I heard the word *celebrity* used in a Christian environment, and it was used in regard to myself. I was appalled. I came home, cried for three days, battled things out with the Lord, and came to the conclusion that if I for one moment started to believe that I was a celebrity, I was on my way to grave trouble.

David and I have talked many times about the subtle temptations that exist in public ministry. While there are many people who minister worthily, all too many others have succumbed to these temptations. Some have forgotten that they are ministers of the gospel and begin to view themselves as entertainers. They refuse to speak without receiving fat fees, to travel unless they go first class; some have even been known to require a road manager who travels with them arranging for luggage and shielding them from an over-eager public. For some, it seems that the standards of Hollywood too often become the measurement for Christian ministry.

A conversation was reported to me recently between a couple of these "personalities" who were discussing what kind of refreshments should be served at conferences—"Oh, you have to serve coffee," one said and the other agreed. "It's a known fact that more books are bought when people have had coffee."

When I hear reports like this and then examine my own heart and find similar disturbing thoughts . . . when my own priorities become muddy, I've learned to make Christ my standard for service. *What would Christ feel if he were party to a conversation like this? What would Christ's instructions be regarding hon-*

orarium schedules? What would Christ say regarding certain Christian publishers' space advertisements which seem to be creating celebrity personna? Somehow I can't see my Lord engaging in a modern-day conversation about the beneficial effect of caffeine in stimulating religious book sales.

Christ himself understood the dangers of the Christian ministry circuit those two thousand years ago when he sent out his young disciples, all raring to try out their new spiritual powers. Mark 6:7-9 says,

> Calling the Twelve to him, he sent them out two by two and gave them authority over evil spirits. These were his instructions: "Take nothing for the journey except a staff—no bread, no bag, no money in your belts. Wear sandals but not an extra tunic."

In other words, he imposed upon them outward disciplines—neediness, economic dependency—in order to remind them that they were ministering on his behalf. It's hard to give way to an overactive ego when you're wearing the same dusty outer garment, soiled with travel and smelling with journey sweat. It's hard to forget the real purpose of itinerant ministry when there are no guarantees of even the creature comforts: a bed, a crust of bread, a warm meal.

When the disciples came back from these journeys into the countryside exclaiming, "Lord, even the demons submit to us in your name," the Lord immediately turned their attention to what was of primary importance, "However, do not rejoice that the spirits submit to you, but rejoice that your names are written in heaven" (Luke 10:17, 20). Christ knew that the most dangerous power in the world is authentic spiritual power.

Consequently, he taught his disciples an odd little parable which is recorded in Luke 17:

> Suppose one of you had a servant plowing or looking after the sheep. Would he say to the servant when he comes in from the field, "Come along now and sit down to eat"? Would he not rather say,

> "Prepare my supper, . . . after that you may eat and drink"? So you also, when you have done everything you were told to do, should say, "We are unworthy servants; we have only done our duty" (17:7-8, 10).

Now that's what I call the cold water effect. The phrase, "I am an unworthy servant; I have only done my duty" helps calm my vaulting ego when I return home from meetings a little heady about the way I feel God has just used me.

Christ imposes outward disciplines that help protect his servants from pride in Christian service. And we must learn to impose similar disciplines upon ourselves as we work in union with him toward our own personal spiritual maturity.

In the Fall of 1984 I took a week's retreat in a little cottage in the mountains of California. I was all alone; and I spent the week in silence, in prayer, in fasting, in putting myself aside so I could hear the Lord if he chose to speak to my heart. In the quiet of that week, I felt as though Christ imposed one of those outward disciplines upon me. I was deeply impressed not to take honorariums for the meetings I had already accepted for the next year, 1985. I was obedient, keeping that vow before the Lord; but believe me, it was hard, particularly with the reoccurring bills for two college students.

The first time I spoke knowing I would receive no monies in return for leaving home and for giving four days of exhausting service and for sleeping on a lumpy pull-out couch and for sharing the bathroom with my hostess' five darling daughters, I stood on the platform and my heart began to sing the words of that ancient Latin poem—*te Deum! te Deum!*—To God! To God!

And I felt strangely freed to do the work of the Lord, to do it for him alone, not for the money in return, nor for human praise and approval. I found untold freedom in acknowledging that I was simply an unworthy servant who was only doing my duty. J. S. Bach, the genius of classical music, must have understood this freedom principle. He regularly dedicated his manuscripts to God with the signature initials "SDG"—*Soli Deo Gloria* (Glory to God alone).

We are so capable of corruption that even our service for God can become a source for pride. We need to learn to allow Christ to help us keep our fists tightly clenched upon humility. You may not be a public speaker (or even want to be one!) but in your own sphere of Christian service there will be subtle influences tempting you in ways large and small to sell your soul. An unthanked mother tempted by attitude martyrdom; an organizational wizard tempted to preen too much because of the latest all-church activity successfully implemented; the women's fellowship leader who has mapped out "the most successful ever" missionary fund-raising project; the organist expecting commendation regarding the magnificent music created each Sunday—we must all remember why we are serving and for whom our service is being expanded. If we don't, we will eventually find ourselves inside a prison looking out, not exactly sure of our crime.

Have you ever been in prison?

I don't know why, but prisons have always fascinated me. For years I've read the prison literature of the world—a few sociological dissertations on the rationales for crime and punishment, but mostly the work of dissidents jailed for their political beliefs or of prisoners-of-war imprisoned in labor camps or of innocent Christians kept behind bars because of their faith. I (and a few of my friends) have waded through all the volumes of Solzhenitsyn's *Gulag Archipelago.* I've interviewed students in the Middle East who gave testimony of imprisonment and torture. I worked for three quarters of a year on a book (never published) about a missionary imprisoned during the Second World War in a Japanese POW camp. I've written down the testimony of Southeast Asian refugees, many of whom stated that Vietnam, for instance, had become a gigantic prison and that the Communists were the most cruel wardens in man's history.

I have a sweet-as-honey southern friend who conducts weekly meetings for feminine inmates in a federal prison. She had obtained, with some difficulty, special permission for me to visit women who were on a retreat of another sort than the kind at which I usually speak.

I remember well those women inmates—their aimlessness, the darkness in some of their eyes, the confusion in the demeanor of others, the outright flirtatiousness of one with the male warden who walked us in. I remember thinking, *O Lord, what favors are being traded in a place like this?* I also remember discovering that my sweet-as-honey southern friend had iron in her soul which was not readily discerned by the outward eye. "That gal we just talked to," she whispered. "She's here because she murdered her own baby." It took spiritual courage for her to minister in this place.

On this visitation afternoon I watched as children were cleared by the security check and then rushed to hug their mothers whose lives were being lived out behind electrical fences. I wondered how a mother faces her child when she knows the child has to tell someone, "I'm going to visit my mother today; she's in a high security federal prison." Watching that greeting between child and inmate mother (one of the women was in advanced pregnancy) was a moment of intense incongruity for me.

Prisons are terrible places; the stories of torture behind them have a haunting redundancy. There is a banal evil mind behind man's inhumanity to man; freedom beats hard in the breast of almost every human.

Why is it, then, that so many Christians carry their own prisons on their backs? We allow ourselves to be imprisoned by the past, by our own fatal flaws, by hatred and misunderstanding of other humans, by lust for things or positions or recognitions. And by far, one of the greatest of human bondages has to be our bondage to human approval. This bondage is so subtle that we often don't know we've allowed opinion to become our jailer or praise to become the tag on the key that has locked us in this cell.

We can often identify friends who've walked into this jail and locked the door. We watch them work hard for public recognition—we might even see them sell pieces of their soul for favors from the warden. They prostitute their integrity for the head place at a dignitary's table or a special speaking position or in order to see their name published in a donor's list or an article on their ministry featured in a Christian magazine.

We can always see another person's jail. What's difficult is identifying the length and breadth of our own cell. I discovered the nature of the prison I was carrying on my own back when I realized I was hurt when just a few people read the books that I had labored hard over. I was hurt when I received no recognition from literary peers, those people whose writing I admired and whose opinions I valued. And actually, none of these things are bad in themselves—it's just that when we want them too much, the jailer's key turns the tumblers and bolts on the cell door and we find ourselves locked inside.

So I began to attempt to do my work for Christ alone. I refused honorariums for a year and followed harder after him. I ventured into harder and more arduous prayer exercises and purposely neglected to mention my journeys to friends. I practiced doing secret acts of Christian love, small gifts and kindnesses for others, without signing my name or without pointing to my own benevolences. I prepared dinners for guests as though I was cooking food for one Guest alone. I learned to look to him for his approval and to be content with his words, "Well done."

Through these small acts of renunciation, my prison doors finally flew open, the bonds that had been tightening around my heart fell away and I walked out of the cell an unworthy servant who was only doing her duty—but a free woman at last.

Will you join me? This inner freedom is one of the most exciting liberations a woman can have. But you must first begin to identify the prison of human approval in which you are jailed; and then you must turn your heart toward his approval, the only key that can turn the tumblers of the locked padlock on your cell.

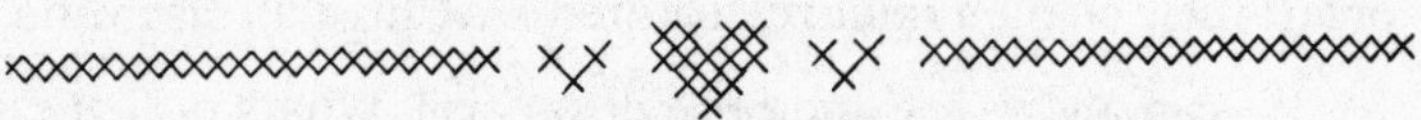

The Freedom Prayer

Lord, I renounce my desire for human praise,
For the approval of my peers,
The need for public recognition.
I deliberately put these aside today,
Content to hear you whisper
Well done, my faithful servant.
Amen.

The Discipline of Choosing Freedom from the Need for Human Approval

Suggested passages for study and meditation: Pride—Jeremiah 9:23-24; 2 Corinthians 11:16-12:10; Ezekial 28:1-10; Proverbs 16:18. Living for God's approval rather than man's—Acts 4:1-20; Daniel 3; John 5:30, 6:38; 12:37-43.

Hymns for meditation: "O Jesus, I Have Promised"
"Take My Life and Let It Be"
"Let God Be God"
"I'd Rather Have Jesus"

I believe God wants to teach me more about choosing freedom from the need for human approval because:

This concept is not new; I have previously learned something about living before God alone when:

The Scripture(s) God is impressing upon my heart that underscores this discipline is written out below.

What this Scripture means in terms of my personal situation is:

Other incidents have come to bear on my learning process: I have read something in a book; a friend spoke a pertinent word; my memory was jogged about an almost forgotten event. Such additional experiences are:

As an indication of my intent to develop this inner discipline, I will pray "The Freedom Prayer." I have prayed the prayer (circle the appropriate numbers):

Seven days, twice a day

1 2 3 4 5 6 7 8 9 10 11 12 13 14

Thirty days, once a day

1 2 3 4 5 6 7 8 9 10 11 12 13 14

15 16 17 18 19 20 21 22 23 24 25 26 27 28 29 30

During the above learning time frame, the friend I will share this learning process with is:

11

NO EXITS:

The Discipline of Looking for a Door in Closed Places

It all began so innocently. I was a guest speaker for a summer conference on a midwestern campus. My first lecture was scheduled for 9:30 in the morning; but upon arrival I learned I was expected to lead a creative worship experience. I estimated I had about two hours of work ahead of me. I needed to call home for some quotes, type and xerox an "order of service" handout, and finalize my thoughts for my speech, which now needed to be adapted. My hostess, the dean of women, kindly lent me her key to the administration offices; and just to make certain I had enough time, I rose early, wrapped myself in a shawl for the cool morning, made my way across the unfamiliar campus carrying two Bibles (different versions), a thesaurus, a hymnal, a large anthology of poetry, and my briefcase.

The campus was visually confusing to me. Some gifted architect had designed buildings of superb form which were, nevertheless, almost impossible for the newcomer to tell one from another. After a few false turns, I finally let myself into what I thought was the backside of the administration building. I heard a bell ringing and the door slammed shut behind me; I turned and noticed with dismay a large sign warning, FIRE EXIT. USE ONLY IN CASE OF EMERGENCY. VIOLATORS WILL BE PROSECUTED.

Visions of a bell clanging in a switch box in some nearby police or fire department flashed in my head. How was I supposed to know the door was a fire exit? There were no signs posted outside (but then most students wouldn't be carrying the master key to the campus, would they?). Well, at least the ringing had stopped, and I was finally inside, somewhere in the basement. All I had to do was make my way through the dimly lit corridors to the front of the building where I would certainly find familiar stairs and the familiar lobby from last night's meeting.

It wasn't long, however, before I discovered I had unlocked the door to the wrong building. I was lost inside the imposing, sacrosanct graduate library. Stacks and stacks of books lined rows and rows of shelves. More warnings assaulted my eye. AUTHORIZED PERSONNEL ALLOWED HERE ONLY! THE WARNHOUSE COLLECTION IS OPEN ONLY TO THOSE WHO HAVE RECEIVED THE LIBRARIAN'S PERMISSION! Oh, an empty, forbidding library at 6 o'clock in the morning is as deathly quiet as a cemetery.

To make a long story short, I wandered in that library for an hour trying to find a way out. I kept thinking I would certainly come to the front door—but I never did find it in my whole hour of frantic wanderings. I only discovered more fire exits with dire threats of prosecution and elevators that landed me in corridors that went nowhere. There were even doors that taunted me with freedom but only led to second-floor balconies with no staircases downward—the creative architect again! I was so desperate to get out, I seriously considered tossing my books, my thesaurus, my hymnal, my large anthology of poetry, my briefcase, my shawl and high-heeled shoes over the side, then lowering myself to the ground like the stunt men do in cowboy movies—but I knew, with my luck, I'd break an ankle. Then what would I say to my friend, the dean of women?

Finally, fighting the panic and panting like I had been jogging, I retraced my original steps, breathed a prayer, and plunged back through the original fire door I had so innocently entered. The buzzer sounded again. I frantically banged the door behind me in order to silence it, raced up the stairs; and having no intention of facing the fire trucks and police sirens I was convinced would soon be waiting for me, I beat my way out of the vicinity.

Well, the campus was as peaceful as I had left it. Everyone was still asleep, unconcerned and unaware of my terrible little drama. There were no police or firemen to prosecute me because of my naive stupidity. There were only birds singing morning songs and a summer day beginning.

I found the administration building. It was the one next door. Calming my rapidly beating heart, I typed the worship order sheets, duplicated them, found the needed poetry and hymns and Bible passages. I called home for one quote and sympathy from my husband and spent a little time reworking my speech. Precisely at 9:30 that morning I stepped on the platform and addressed the three hundred and some assembled conferees, then led them in a creative worship experience. I did as well as could be expected under the circumstances and no one in that auditorium knew I had experienced one brief, blazing moment when I experientially understood what it is like to have no exit, when irrationally, like a little child, I had wanted to throw back my head and scream, "Open the door! Somebody! Open the door!"

John Paul Sartre, the French humanist philosopher who was noted for propounding the philosophy of existentialism, wrote a play in which he dramatized the modern dilemma of man. The main character is placed in a room without windows or doors. He is unable to escape from himself or from the physical and psychological boundaries of those four walls. Sartre titled the play, *No Exit.*

A young man sat in my home, a living symbol of the dramatist's play. I have seldom seen anyone experiencing such a protracted depression. His whole physical language expressed "dead-end." Even his eyelids were at half-mast. His lifework had become meaningless. There was no decent Christian fellowship available. A series of illnesses and a pattern of broken relationships had led him to despair. He profoundly doubted his own self. Faith had been broken with his soul. Convinced there was no exit, he had come to me hoping I would say differently.

Thoreau has been quoted as believing that most men lead lives of quiet desperation—I have come to think that this is sadly true. When I was young, I used to over-idealize acquaintances. That one was so beautiful or so talented or so perfect or so brilliant. But during our years in the pastorate when people began to share their secret burdens with us, I discovered that the beautiful, the talented, the perfect, and the brilliant often hide their own pains. I learned it was more accurate to assume that people had problems than it was to assume that they didn't.

At some time in life, we all feel the claustrophobic certainty that we are trapped in a room of some kind without windows or doors. There is no escape from the problems besetting us. We are wandering in forbidden territory and some demonically clever architect has filled the maze of life with elevators that lead nowhere, with balconies that have no stairways, and with doors that bear signs threatening prosecution.

I told the young man who sat in my living room what I have often had to remind myself: I don't believe in no exits. I'm aware of danger. I've tasted suffering. And I'm familiar with dreadful circumstances—but rooms without windows and doors? My library excursion aside, that is beyond my frame of reference.

"How can this be?" someone asks, thinking of that husband who is the jailer in a brutal marital relationship. "Who do you think you are?" someone wonders, holding the little infant the doctors have prognosticated will never be normal. "If you had to face the things I face . . ." says another, dreading the daily grind of boring work, poverty, and physical exhaustion.

Let me carefully explain: There are circumstances which *seem* to be dead ends. But I believe in a God who fills the human heart with hope when all the world proclaims there is no reason for hoping. I said to my young male friend, "There are times in our lives when circumstances have brought us to a point where we can scarcely believe, not with our tongues or our hearts or our minds. At these times we need a believer to cross our paths, someone who can believe for us for a while, someone who can gently and kindly remind us how to believe again."

There have been times in my life when others have believed for me until I was whole enough to take up the banner myself; there are times when I have waved the banner over others.

How we hate closed doors, whether we need to get out or whether we need to get in.

Have you ever been locked out of your house? I have quite a history of this, stretching all the way back to childhood. One frustrating incident that occurred frequently after I was married was when my husband, who is an extremely sound sleeper, would go to bed early, and I would return from a late night church function only to discover that the doors had been locked.

I would stand on the little front porch of our home and ring the doorbell . . . and ring . . . and ring. Then in a stage whisper (so that the neighbors wouldn't be chuckling over the fact that the pastor had locked out the pastor's wife again) I would call, "David! David! David!"

No answer.

Our bedroom was directly above the front porch, and my next point of strategy was to toss wood chips against it hoping that the noise would rouse my husband; when this proved fruitless, I finally was forced to march across the street to sympathetic members of our church who would not immediately attribute my plight to marital discord. In their home I would phone my husband (the phone was on the stand right by the bedside), "David. I'm locked out again. Will you please come down and open the front door."

Then, being barely civil to my rescuers, I would race across the street because David would often roll over and go back to sleep, forcing me to repeat the doorbell ringing, the standing on the front porch and calling *soto voce*, the throwing of wood chips, and again dashing across to my neighbors, who by this time had become greatly exercised in hilarity.

It's terrible to be locked out, no matter how funny it sounds. It is also terrible to be locked in.

Time magazine carried a short article about David Tom, a frail young Chinese immigrant who was first admitted to an Illinois mental institute in 1952. The only English words he could say were, "Me no crazy. This nuthouse." No one listened to him. Worse, he was never examined by anyone who could speak Chinese. Nearly three decades went by before anyone even tried to understand.

In 1978, a social worker took Tom to a Chinese restaurant where he had a conversation in the Cantonese dialect with the cook. The cook told the hospital staff there was nothing wrong with Tom, setting in motion a four-year battle in the state courts to win his release. Tom's long nightmare had begun when, suffering from tuberculosis, he was admitted to a sanatorium. Because what he said seemed incomprehensible, he was later diagnosed as a retarded schizophrenic.

At the age of fifty-four, David Tom was finally released from the Illinois State Psychiatric Institute in Chicago. Tom and his brother Richard entered the U.S. in 1951 as illegal aliens. Richard testified in the court case that he knew his brother was not insane, but he did not step forward to help David because he feared deportation.

Stories like this always evoke an instinctive reaction of horror in the reader; we all have a fear of the no exit places of life. Each of us intuitively understand that life is a house of bondage, and a rash or violent indiscrimination can make any of us its next prisoner.

But I am a believer. I can testify that there is a Door to this house of bondage called Life; Moses foretold this door in Exodus 12 when he told the elders of Israel to:

> Go at once and select the animals for your families and slaughter the Passover lamb. Take a bunch of hyssop, dip it into the blood in the basin and put some of the blood on the top and on both sides of the doorframe (12:21-22).

Christ's hands stretch to the doorposts; his head touches the lintel. And it is his blood spread on the wood through which we must walk in order to find deliverance from the seemingly windowless, exitless places of life.

In his gospel, John underscores the great "I am" sayings of Christ. Each of these sayings speaks to a deep universal longing in the human soul, and Christ promises that he, himself, is the fulfillment of these longings. "I am the Bread of Life" speaks to the spiritual starvation each one of us discovers at some time in our journey; "I am the Vine" speaks of the longing for joining with another on the deepest level of intimacy.

"I am the Door," says Christ. In a sense, at least at some time in life, we are all like the David Toms of this world imprisoned in a house of bondage that keeps us from going to the place where we belong. Unwhole relationships, illness, or emotional deprivation is our meager prison fare. We stand on the threshold, banging on the locked door, calling "Let me in! Let me in!" Or we are imprisoned behind a locked door, trying to cope with the overwhelming stress of life's lunacy and crying "Let me out! Let me out!" Each of us in our own way needs a door opened so that we may escape this house of bondage.

Christ says, "I am the door; if anyone enters through Me, he shall be saved and shall go in and out" (John 10:9 NAS).

What is the house of bondage that imprisons you?

No Exits

Is it pride, that old animal as ancient as the Garden of Eden, that whispers in your ear, "You don't need anybody else; you can do it on your own, don't ask for help, don't ever ask for help"? Now you stand before a locked door and the key of pride has proven to be inadequate in turning the tumblers.

Is it depression, self-pity, resentment? Now you stand before a door which is bolted, and you are excluded, shut away.

Not only are you locked in/locked out with a closed door slammed shut, barred, and barricaded; you are now beyond belief. You need someone to believe a little while for you until your own faith system is restored.

I believe. I believe in the One who opens all locked doors, the One who said he was the Door, the One whose body is stretched in invitation, beneath which we must pass if we are to escape our confinement, and through whom we must pass if we are to go in and out.

Perhaps my belief can reach across these pages and touch your heart just enough so that you will begin to believe again.

The Prayer for Open Doors

I refuse to believe in dead ends and no exits.
Particularly when your head touches the lintel
and your arms stretch to the doorposts
and your blood marks the wood.

I choose to believe that you are the Door
that opens. I choose to believe that you are the Way
along which we must pass.
I choose to believe.
Help my unbelief, I pray.
Amen.

The Discipline of Looking for a Door in Closed Places

Suggested passages for study and meditation: Isaiah 40:28-31; Jeremiah 32:26-27; Genesis 18:14; Matthew 19:26; Mark 10:27; Luke 18:27; 1 Corinthians 10:13; 2 Peter 2:9

Hymns for meditation: "Through the Love of God Our Savior, All Will Be Well"
"Come Ye Disconsolate"
"All the Way My Savior Leads Me"
"He Giveth More Grace"

I believe God wants to teach me more about looking for a door in closed places because:

This concept is not new; I previously learned something about faith when:

The Scripture(s) God is impressing upon my heart that underscores this discipline is written out below.

What this Scripture means in terms of my personal situation is:

Other incidents have come to bear on my learning process: I have read something in a book; a friend spoke a pertinent word; my memory was jogged about an almost forgotten event. Such additional experiences are:

As an indication of my intent to develop this inner discipline, I will pray "The Prayer for Open Doors." I have prayed the prayer

(circle the appropriate numbers):

Seven days, twice a day

1 2 3 4 5 6 7 8 9 10 11 12 13 14

Thirty days, once a day

1 2 3 4 5 6 7 8 9 10 11 12 13 14

15 16 17 18 19 20 21 22 23 24 25 26 27 28 29 30

During the above learning time frame, the friend I will share this learning process with is:

12

HANDMAIDENS:

The Discipline of Offering Myself Up

I love the cry of Mary, the mother of Jesus, confronted in that awesome moment by the angel Gabriel. He says to her,

> Rejoice, highly favored one, the Lord is with you; Do not be afraid, Mary, for you have found favor with God. And behold, you will conceive in your womb and bring forth a Son, and shall call His name JESUS.

And she responds,

> Behold, the handmaid of the Lord; be it unto me according to thy word" (Luke 1:26-38 NKJV, KJV).

The word *handmaiden* is also used by Mary in her remarkable prayer "The Magnificat," which is considered classic spiritual literature. "My soul doth magnify the Lord, and my spirit hath rejoiced in God my Savior, for he hath regarded the low estate of his handmaiden." The forty-eighth verse of Luke 1, "He hath regarded the low estate of his handmaiden" is translated this way in the New International version: "For he has been mindful of the humble state of his servant."

This attitude seems to be central to Mary's acceptance of the holy impregnation she experienced. It was an attitude that was key to the grace she displayed throughout Scripture despite the shame, the confusion, or the agony she experienced being the mother of the Messiah. This attitude should be sought as well by all Christians, men and women, today.

How do we do this—we, the women of this modern world? How do we interpret the meaning of the concept of being a servant? We may have a college girl who cleans for us once a week as she works her way through school; some of us may be fortunate to employ a hire-a-maid service. We may make weekly trips to the dry cleaners, or we may even be able to coerce our teens into cleaning out the garage as they search for ways to make extra money. But servants?—real, live people who exist to carry out our desires and commands? Servants are an anachronism in our twentieth-century, do-it-yourself culture.

What is a servant? The Old Testament Scriptures give us clues to what Mary was saying. Handmaidens were of the lower class. The synonyms used interchangeably throughout Scripture give an indication of this: handmaid, maid, maidservant, slavegirl, bondwoman, bondmaid. The bondmaid was owned by her master or mistress. Her life was bought at a price, and she was willing to do whatever was required of her without question. There is a chilling record in Judges 19 of the concubine who was offered to the base men of the city of Gibeah to sate their physical lust; and without a doubt, this has to be one of the most unspeakably horrible stories in all the Bible. But in its extremity, it illustrates the position of the bondmaid.

Handmaidens were childbearers, lifebearers. Rachel and Leah's maids, Zilpah and Bilhah, bore children for their mistresses in times of their barrenness. Hagar became pregnant after Sarah grew weary waiting for the fulfillment of God's promise and legally offered her slave to her husband Abraham. (Her impatience created the roots of an internecine nationalist struggle from which our modern world suffers.)

Female slaves, although owned by their masters, were subject to specific law and custom; they weren't simply victim to their owner's whims and fancies. A chief wife's servant-maid might bear children of the master. But under the law, if a Hebrew girl was sold as a slave, even in the context of the Old Testament polygamous culture, her marital status was carefully guarded. She might marry her master or his son or become a properly maintained concubine; but if the master failed to implement any of the above choices, she could go free by law. If she refused her freedom, she was marked for life by having an awl driven through her earlobe against a doorpost.

So what did Mary mean when she replied, "Be it unto me according to thy word, I am a handmaiden of the Lord"?

The word *handmaid*, or the various forms of it, is used fifty-five times in the Old Testament. Rachel and Leah, Bathsheba, Ruth and Sarah were not handmaidens, but they referred to themselves as such to express humility before men of stature or in relation to their own great husbands. For instance, in 1 Kings, Bathsheba referred to herself as a handmaid to David.

Perhaps one of the loveliest references to handmaidens is in the love story of Ruth and Boaz. According to Levitical law, when a woman was widowed without children, her husband's next of male kin was to marry her and attempt to provide a child that would be counted as the heir of the dead husband. But the drama that Ruth enacts on the threshing floor in the middle of the night (coached, interestingly enough, by her own mother-in-law, Naomi) is more than a formality reminding Boaz, the almost-next-of-kin, of his office. I think it was also a love offering. Ruth speaks when he awakens and wonders who is beside him, "I am Ruth thine handmaid: spread therefore thy skirt over thine handmaid; for thou art a near kinsman" (Ruth 3:9, KJV). Was this a moment of social courtesy or legal ritual? Hardly. She was offering herself, body and soul, to her lord.

Was Mary's expression superficial humility? Again, I think not. She was offering herself, body and soul, to her Lord so that she could give birth to something holy.

So must we, modern women that we are, learn to become handmaidens of the Lord. It is not until we offer ourselves up completely, not until we give up our rights, not until we seek first the will of this Divine Lord, that we can know the meaning of giving birth to holy things—whether the children of our hearts or minds or hands.

Being a servant is one of the most important lessons for Christians to learn; but unfortunately, we often have to work through gross misconceptions. We have fears about entrusting ourselves to any boss; but we must learn in our spiritual journey that this Master is unlike any other. He will not abuse us or misuse us. He has our greatest interest at heart. He encourages us through our servanting to be all that we can be and then gives us his own Holy Spirit to empower us to become so. This master is one who even laid down his life for those who were his servants.

He is a Master unlike any other. Not to be feared, he is worthy of our service.

Many of us think servanting means losing ourselves in such a way that we become people without personality, people without original thinking ability, people without giftedness. But when one serves this Master, the opposite is true: He makes us full, complete human beings filled with his own image, with his own amazing mentality. Paradoxically, while teaching us to be more like him, we become more of whom he created us to be.

Look again at Mary. There's a revealing incident about her in the story of Christ's first miracle, at the wedding feast in Cana of Galilee where Jesus turned the water into wine. Jesus' mother was a guest, and Jesus and his disciples were invited too. The wine supply ran out during the festivities, and Mary came to her son with the problem.

"I can't help you now," he said. "It isn't yet time for showing who I am."

Now despite this disclaimer, the scriptural narrative tells us that Mary looked at the servants and told them, "Do whatever he tells you!"

I love it! Having sons myself, I can picture what may have happened: The exchanged glances between mother and son, the long looks as Mary puts her son on the spot, the prototypical Jewish mother! Her thinking is almost implied: *Well, he may be God's Son, the Holy Spirit may be his Father; but after all, I had a thing or two to do with this young man. My friends are in an embarrassing situation, and I know that this son of mine can help them out.* (Long look to Christ.) Then to the servants a command to obey him. This was a woman, as submissive as she was to the work of God, who was also fully human: not quite sure her miraculously-conceived child had understood the imperative of human need.

Old Elizabeth, miraculously pregnant with the child who would be the prophet about whom Christ himself declared: "No greater man was born of woman than John!"—old Elizabeth says to the young Mary before these two incredible birthings, "You believed that God would do what He said; that is why he has given you this wonderful blessing."

Mary was not randomly chosen to be the recipient of holy favor; God knew she had potential to submit and potential to believe. Mary not only believed that God would send his Messiah, she believed the words of the angel Gabriel that she was to be the mother of that promised child. She also believed that the same child, her son, was capable of helping her embarrassed friends, even though miracles were not slated yet on the godly agenda.

Mary was a handmaiden of the Lord, a mixture of holiness and humanity. We must put away the fear that serving this Master is predicated upon the loss of our humanity. We become more human, more like Christ's prototype of humanity, when we become slaves of God. Paul asks in Romans 6:16-18,

> Don't you know that when you offer yourselves to someone to obey him as slaves, you are slaves to the one whom you obey—whether you are slaves to sin, which leads to death, or to obedience, which leads to righteousness? But thanks be to God that, though you used to be slaves to sin, you wholeheartedly obeyed the form of teaching to which you were entrusted. You have been set free from sin and have become slaves to righteousness.

And what happens when we become slaves of God? Like Mary, a miracle birth occurs. For in truth when women offer themselves up as handmaidens, bondwomen, slavegirls to this most wonderful Master, they too will give birth to a holy thing. Through the overpowering of the Holy Spirit, we are implanted with the very personality and life and mind of Jesus Christ.

We must learn to offer ourselves up!

This is one of the meanings of nativity. Let us not limit nativity to a Babe wailing piteously on the straw, or to one season of the year. Nativity occurs in each of us who, like Mary, believes, in each one of us who implores our Lord to do unto us according to his word. His life is incarnated over and over again in us.

We must learn to offer ourselves up.

We must listen to the voice of a holy one, startling and unexpected, saying, "Blessed art thou among men, among women." We must have the courage to respond, "I am a handmaiden of the Lord. Be it unto me according to thy word."

We must give birth, and then we discover that the work of our hands, the work of our minds, the work of our hearts—these have become holy children who make their way in this unholy world, doing most holy acts.

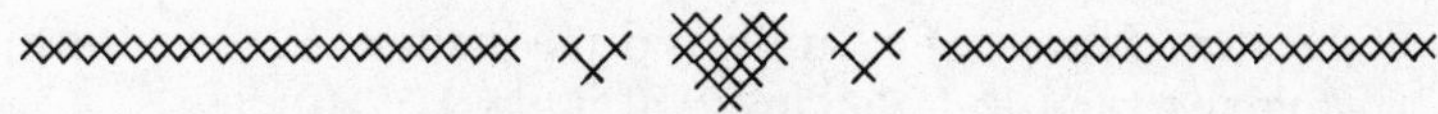

The Handmaiden Prayer

My dear Master,
I give to you all that I am
for you to do in me all that you would
so that I may, filled with your will,
do in the world all that I should.
Amen.

The Discipline of Offering Myself up

Suggested passages for study and meditation: Esther; Ruth; Romans 12: 1-8; Galatians 2:20; Luke 17:7-10, 33.

Hymns for meditation: "Only One Life"
"With Eternity's Values in View"
"I'll Live for Him"
"Living for Jesus"

I believe God wants to teach me more about offering up myself because:

This concept is not new; I have previously learned something about this discipline when:

The Scripture(s) God is impressing upon my heart that underscores this discipline is written out below.

What this Scripture means in terms of my personal situation is:

Other incidents have come to bear on my learning process: I have read something in a book; a friend spoke a pertinent word; my memory was jogged about an almost forgotten event. Such additional experiences are:

As an indication of my intent to develop this inner discipline, I will pray "The Handmaiden Prayer." I have prayed the prayer

(circle the appropriate numbers):

Seven days, twice a day

1 2 3 4 5 6 7 8 9 10 11 12 13 14

Thirty days, once a day

1 2 3 4 5 6 7 8 9 10 11 12 13 14

15 16 17 18 19 20 21 22 23 24 25 26 27 28 29 30

During the above learning time frame, the friend I will share this learning process with is:

13

VIGILS FOR NATIVITY:

The Discipline of Watching for Christ in the World

The first time I was in Bethlehem was in 1978. It was a hot October day; David, Randy, and I had just stepped off a bus along with forty of our new Jewish friends from the El Al tour we three Gentiles had crashed—a ten-day excursion through Israel. Together, we shuffled through the dust to the keyhole door of the old church through which pilgrims must bow if they are to enter the old sanctuary. Slipping through the opening, we adjusted our sight to the musty shadows within while our Israeli guide, a sabra (Israeli-born), a nationalist, attempted to explain the Christian meaning of Bethlehem to his group—all Jewish but ourselves.

We descended the winding side stairs to the grotto which tradition holds to be the birthplace of Christ. I was almost disgusted by the ardor of certain pilgrims (none of them in our group) who tearfully kissed the ornate brass star in the floor which supposedly marks the very spot of nativity. I can remember thinking indignantly, *There is nothing holy about these holy shrines, nothing holy at all!*

The second time I visited Bethlehem everything was different. Perhaps this was because I was in Bethlehem on Epiphany, the day when Orthodox Christian churches celebrate the birth of Christ.

Epiphany means a revealing of truth. In literature we call a story which has a point of truth so powerful that the hero or heroine is altered by that truth—we call this an epiphanal story. The Greek root word, *epiphaneia*, means "an appearance." Webster's dictionary defines epiphany as: 1) an appearance or apparition of a deity or other supernatural being, and 2) the twelfth day after Christmas, January 6, in commemoration of the revealing of Jesus as the Christ to the Gentiles in the persons of the Magi; sometimes called Twelfth Night.

So I was in Bethlehem on the night of revealing, an evening of appearance. This time my traveling companions were a group of Christians, a study tour of religious leaders invited to survey the trauma of the Middle East for the purpose of becoming educated about all sides of the tragic dilemma. We had interviewed Jordanian government officials, PLO leaders, Israeli Knesset politicians. We had listened to the explanations of citizens and civilians and students, the businessman, the laborer, and the artisan. We would meet with Greek Orthodox church leaders, the Grand Mufti of Lebanon, the monks in the University of the Holy Spirit above Beirut, the newly-appointed Cardinal of Lebanon, Antoine Pierre Khoraiche, Patriarch of the Maronite Rite. We would talk with U.S. Embassy officials, tour the PLO camps, and eventually end our journey in the palace at Amman in a private interview with Queen Noor and King Hussein of Jordan. It was an experience that most of us would never live again, one that has taken me years just to begin to absorb the tearing passions and despairs and hatreds and poignancies.

Bethlehem, about a half hour drive from Jerusalem, was scheduled for the midpoint of our travel itinerary. An Arab community on the West Bank, it is under Israeli army occupation. Military checkpoints mark the road from Jerusalem to Bethlehem. We parked in the dark on the edge of the little town; then walked, taking bracing breaths of the clear winter air, toward the military checkpoint through which all pilgrims to the birthplace would have to pass that Christmas night.

Young Israeli soldiers wearing khaki uniforms, boots, and warm khaki jackets patrolled the streets; and all, even the young women, carried automatic rifles. *Ah, this is the way it was the night Christ was born,* I thought. Then too, there was a military occcupation and a ferment of partisan unrest.

We entered the checkpoint and submitted to the search for concealed weapons. The Israeli soldier searching me, a young woman, yawned. "I'm sorry you have to be here tonight," I said, smiling at her and meaning my words in more ways than one. "So am I," she answered, finishing her yawn. "Have a merry Christmas."

"Same to you," I replied without thinking, a habit that can get you into grave trouble in the hot spots of the world if you don't learn to be careful. Then I laughed, "But this isn't your holiday. . . ."

"Not at all," she laughed back, motioning me on through. "Not at all."

I stepped into the square. It seemed larger than I had remembered, cleaner. Perhaps it was the absence of hot summer dust or the aimlessness of crowds of tourists pushing their way off tour buses, but the fountain in the square in the middle of Bethlehem seemed new, or at least I hadn't remembered it from before. Again, Israeli soldiers stood in clusters. A large tank loomed imposingly to one side with soldiers atop it. Soldiers with automatic rifles were positioned at watchpoints high in some of the buildings.

"Last year," a companion whispered to me, "the Israelis placed soldiers in the window arches inside the old church. There had been recent riots and they weren't taking any chances with the crowds."

This is not just a money-making tourist zone, I thought. *It's a reenactment of another time, history circling round in its crazy carnival ride.* The ancient words I had memorized as a teen echoed in my memory: "Then Herod, when he saw that he was deceived by the wise men, was exceedingly angry; and he sent forth and put to death all the male children who were in Bethlehem and all its districts, from two years old and under." Bethlehem has ever been neighbor to violence.

Something significant was happening in Bethlehem on this night. My own instincts that police the environments in which I find myself were suddenly on watchful alert.

We went into the Church of the Nativity, passing through another checkpoint and bending at the now familiar keyhole door. This time I was not a tourist with a skeptic's heart, but a pilgrim bringing eager expectation to Bethlehem, bringing readiness to bow in worship on this evening in advent.

Far from being a musty mausoleum of tradition, with hot, stale air and bored attendants, the old church was alive. Christians with Arab faces were bowing to worship, submitting to a humiliating search at the checkpoints, and bending at the keyhole door in order to enter. They, like myself, were coming to Bethlehem on the evening of Epiphany.

I watched as beautiful antique brass lanterns hung on garlands of wire were lowered on pulleys, then lighted, then lifted aloft, dancing in motion and spangling the aisle and the nave and the altar with diamonds of light.

The Orthodox priests in long black cassocks lit the candles on the altar, young attendants—boys really—appeared wearing crimson. Then the mysterious wail of the Eastern church's liturgy began to rise in Aramaic song, like a low moan out of the Moabite mountains, like the wind blowing through the land, like an ancient memory of old, old prayer. The great vault of the church filled with sound, and I felt sure that I could soon absorb the meaning of the liturgical chant if I but listened long enough.

At that moment the bells outside and above the church began to sound and the whole old place reverberated with echoes. Gong! Gong! Gong! I felt like my whole being rose in praise, caught in this uncanny juxtaposition of sound, the liturgical wail and the iron bells calling. I, a human clapper, lifted my heart in adoring rhyme: Gong! Gong! Gong! He is born! Tell! Tell!

And the worshippers continued to come, to make their way through the military checkpoints without so that they could enter into the heart of the birthplace within.

I know next to nothing about Eastern Orthodoxy, and I am an absolute novice at high church liturgy. My Aramaic consists of knowing only two expressions of greeting, *sallom alekom* and *marhabah*—but I know a holy moment when I am in the midst of it. I may have been the only one who saw the appearing, but despite the agony of the world without, despite the passions and the hatreds—Israeli against Palestinian, Jew against Arab, neighbor against neighbor—Christ, the one for whose birth the bells were ringing, Christ had revealed himself for those with hearts to see on this evening of Epiphany, January 6, 1983.

I sat for a while as the service at the altar continued, then I slipped down the crooked stairway to the grotto, the place where tradition says the Christ child was born. This too was different. On each of the few stairs sat a woman in black, her hair tied beneath a black scarf, long black skirts covering legs and shoes. Some of the faces were young, but most were old, dried by the desert sun and the wind blowing across the wilds, skin wrinkled from deprivation—and each one glanced at me as I walked down as if inquiring, "Have you come to watch with us?" Some smiled. And I looked intently into the shining eyes of each.

The entire grotto was lined with living women's bodies clad in black—sitting, squatting, standing against the wall, some in prayer, some in contemplation; but all waiting in hushed quiet, waiting for the hour of Nativity. And in some way they knew that women all over the world wait for birth, in the morning half- light and in the middle of the night hours, during the day as the clock chimes the hour and the half-hour. We are waiting for the rebirth of creation, for the spiritual nativity of the world.

They were Orthodox nuns (I was told), women who have devoted their lives to prayer.

The grotto itself was alive with light. A multi-tiered brass candelabrum with as many as fifty candles stood to one side of the brass star that marks the place in the floor where pilgrims have touched their lips. And I will tell you the truth, I, a child of the evangelical church, knelt in front of those holy women who watched, and I worshiped in that holy place and my tears fell on the floor.

I climbed back up the stairs, knowing I had been in a place of prayer, a rare experience in my whole church life. One of the men on our church leaders' study tour said to me, "It's beautiful outside. Have you been in the courtyard?" And when I replied that I had not and didn't know how to get there, he led me through a door in the shadows. We were in the courtyard of St. Catherine of Sienna, and we stopped in the winter night beneath the stars that never change, only the gazers who look in wonder upon them. Incongruously, we stood beneath columns of palm trees and beside the beneficent statue of St. Jerome, who translated the Latin Vulgate.

As our heads were tipped to the starry night, the bells began to ring again, to sound over the hills, to pronounce birth in the ears of the Israeli soldiers, to cry in the prisons and hospital wards, to shout nativity even in the streets of Jerusalem. Christ is born! Born! Born! And I realized: There is no peace for the Middle East apart from the forgiveness and redemption given by the Son of God. There is no reconciliation apart from his.

And that moment was lovely, lovely in the night with its ancient echoes of history, lovely in its incongruities; the palms and the winter air, the Jewish soldiers and the statue of a Christian church father—all symbols of the mysteries and multi-paradoxes of faith, confluent complementaries over which my theological self has pondered, stumbled, and finally grown to love. But my heart was really back in the cave, back where the vigil was being kept, back to where the spiritual midwives waited, back to where the candles bloomed waxlight by the birthplace, back to the prayer womb where a place was being reserved for me.

Since this trip to Bethlehem, and perhaps because of it, the Lord has asked me if I will become one of his holy women, if I will become a true woman of prayer—a Protestant nun, if you please. For the first forty years of my life I have been an activist: a church-planter, a child-nurturer, a social-consciousness raiser, an itinerant traveler, a communicator. Prayer has sprung out of my activity and has always competed with it.

Now I am being drawn into the contemplative experience; a learner still, prayer is nevertheless steadily seeping toward the core of my being, the hidden central self I am always at the point of discovering. Activity now must struggle out of prayer and take second place to this more urgent priority.

While teaching a workshop on prayer journaling, I mentioned my novice excursions into intercessory prayer, the few but radical lessons I was learning. A lovely young woman approached me when the session was done. "I experimented with intercessory prayer," she explained. "I found it hard. And painful! Are you finding it painful? I finally had to stop. I'm convinced it could give you wrinkles."

She is right. This kind of prayer, this watching and waiting kind of prayer can give you wrinkles. But I have said Yes. And I have meant it with my whole heart. I would like to be one of those women with craggy faces and shining eyes who watch over Nativity; Christ's birth in each heart; his regeneration in the revival of the church—all the church; his Advent in history, his Second Coming. My goal is to be a wrinkled-faced old woman, and holy.

I am home now and Bethlehem is far away, and each Christmas the soldiers will man the checkpoints again. But the bells of Epiphany ring within each time I pray. And I am keeping vigil for his appearing in the world.

Who will come and watch with me?

The Nativity Prayer of Vigil

Lord,
I give myself to you each day
to keep vigil over your Birth in the world.
Make me into a spiritual midwife, holy;
With wrinkled face, if need be;
But shining eyes,
I pray.
Amen.

THE DISCIPLINE OF WATCHING FOR CHRIST IN THE WORLD

Suggested passages for study and meditation: 1 Thessalonians 5:17; John 17; Colossians 1:9-14; 1 Samuel 12:23; Galatians 6:2.

Hymns for meditation: "Speak, Lord, in the Stillness"
"O Come, O Come, Emmanuel"
"Let All Mortal Flesh Keep Silent"
"Come Thou Long Expected Jesus"

I believe God wants to teach me more about intercessory prayer because:

This concept is not new; I have previously learned something about intercession when:

The Scripture(s) God is impressing upon my heart that underscores this discipline is written out below.

What this Scripture means in terms of my personal situation is:

Other incidents have come to bear on my learning process: I have read something in a book; a friend spoke a pertinent word; my memory was jogged about an almost forgotten event. Such additional experiences are:

As an indication of my intent to develop this inner discipline, I will pray "The Nativity Prayer of Vigil." I have prayed the prayer

(circle the appropriate numbers):

Seven days, twice a day

1 2 3 4 5 6 7 8 9 10 11 12 13 14

Thirty days, once a day

1 2 3 4 5 6 7 8 9 10 11 12 13 14

15 16 17 18 19 20 21 22 23 24 25 26 27 28 29 30

During the above learning time frame, the friend I will share this learning process with is:

The Prayer for Washing

Lord,
I have discovered that I am filthy.
I have not scrubbed enough.
I have not washed thoroughly.
I come before you for cleansing.

Dear Papa,
I confess my dirtiness.
I pray for forgiveness.

Wash me—my hands, my face,
My most hidden inner self.
Make me clean.
Wrap me in the wooly towel of your love.
Let me sit at your table today,
I pray.
Amen.

The Keepin' Talkin' Prayer

Lord,
I promise that to the best of my ability
I will keep talking with you.

I will not let hurts, disappointments, fatigue
or general wretchedness cut me off in communicating
my feelings to you.

Help me to be honest, and help me always to understand that
though there are times I stop talking with you, there are never
times when you stop talking to me.
Amen.

The Prayer for Looking Up

Lord,
Give me the grace to look up,
to be freed from my own image,
from my own mirror-reflection.
Loosen the hold upon me
of many possessions.
Help me to lift my head
and see you.
Fill my vision, I pray.
Amen.

A New Day Prayer

Oh, Lord,
Help me to hold this moment to my heart,
this new day.

Help me to see it as a rare gift of promise,
filled with the potential of living life well,
of remaking old ways new,
of saying Yes to each opportunity, large and small,
of saying Yes to you.

Help me to begin each new day with you in my thoughts,
my first thoughts.

And let me be glad that I have these hours of life to live.
Help me to live them well—now.
Amen.

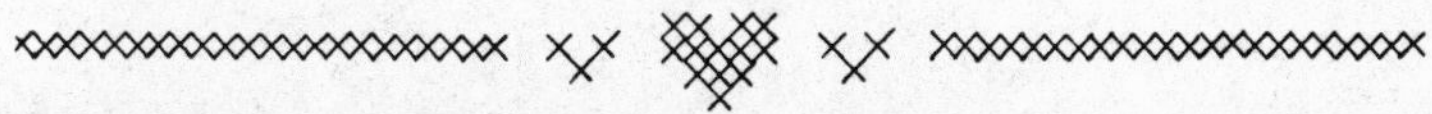

The Prayer for Disappointments

Oh God,
Thank you for the privilege of learning
to know your heart.

Thank you for the parties where nobody comes,
for the empty beds, the tears of alienation.
Thank you for life's disappointments.

Without them I too would fall asleep in your Gethsemane.
Help me to watch.
Help me to watch with you. Help me to use life's pains
redemptively.

I give you my body as a place for your tears.
It is one thing I can do for you.
Amen.

The Christ Betwixt Thee and Me Prayer

Lord,
Be between child and me today,
Between myself and friend.
Hold my hand and the hand of the other also, Christ.
Walk in the middle as we walk.
Be the Word between us as we speak.
Lord, you be at the center of my loves.
Let all others be the radiating circumference.
Christ betwixt thee and me,
Betwixt me and thee, today I pray.
Amen.

The Sacrificing Your Isaac Prayer

Lord,
Here is the work of my mind, my heart, my hand.
Here is the fruit of my womb,
Here is the love of my life.

I lay them on the altar of sacrifice.
I withdraw my hand.
I turn my eyes to your face, my One true God.

I give this cherished thing up to you
the way it was given to me,
with love, with love.
And gladly.
Amen.

The God Hunt Prayer

Lord,
Help me to hunt for you
and find you in my everyday world.
Give me a hunger for yourself
that cannot be satisfied by
any other thing.
Amen.

The Prayer for Being Edited

Lord,
Edit me.
Correct me when my words are faulty.
Revise my thoughts.
Polish the rough passages of my being.

Submit me to a review panel who can judge
my strengths and weaknesses.
Correct the internal rhythm
so that the outward meter will be whole.
I want to be a work of art, Lord, a classic of some kind.

Give me form.
Fill me with the beauty of yourself.
Help those who read my life to see
that you are the workman;
I am the workmanship;
and out of me you are creating a work of art.
Amen.

The Freedom Prayer

Lord, I renounce my desire for human praise,
For the approval of my peers,
The need for public recognition.
I deliberately put these aside today,
Content to hear you whisper
Well done, my faithful servant.
Amen.

The Prayer for Open Doors

I refuse to believe in dead ends and no exits.
Particularly when your head touches the lintel
and your arms stretch to the doorposts
and your blood marks the wood.

I choose to believe that you are the Door
that opens. I choose to believe that you are the Way
along which we must pass.
I choose to believe.
Help my unbelief, I pray.
Amen.

The Handmaiden Prayer

My dear Master,
I give to you all that I am
for you to do in me all that you would
so that I may, filled with your will,
do in the world all that I should.
Amen.

The Nativity Prayer of Vigil

Lord,
I give myself to you each day
to keep vigil over your Birth in the world.
Make me into a spiritual midwife, holy;
With wrinkled face, if need be;
But shining eyes,
I pray.
Amen.